WHEN
I TURNED
NINETEEN

WHEN I TURNED NINETEEN

A VIETNAM WAR MEMOIR

GLYN HAYNIE

When I Turned Nineteen: A Vietnam War Memoir

For information about this title or to order other books
and/or electronic media, contact the publisher:

Glyn Haynie
www.glynhaynie.net
glyn@glynhaynie.com

Library of Congress Control Number:

ISBNs:
Hardback 978-0-9982095-0-0
Paperback 978-0-9982095-1-7
eBook 978-0-9982095-2-4

Printed in the United States of America

Cover design, Interior design, and Editing: 1106 Design, Phoenix AZ
Cover Photograph: Don Ayres
Author Photograph: Shannon Prothro Photography

I dedicate *When I Turned Nineteen: A Vietnam War Memoir* to the First Platoon and the platoon members who did not come home during our 12-month tour.

CONTENTS

ACKNOWLEDGMENTS

The First Platoon and their sacrifices made this book possible. Many platoon members contributed to my story.

Thank you, Mike Dankert, for keeping me straight on most of the events, the Tribute to Peter Zink, and photographs. I would have never finished this book without you. You are my brother.

Thank you to the First Platoon members who contributed:

- ★ John Baxter for sharing letters home, photographs, and contributing to the event "Lieutenant Baxter Gets a Rear Job"
- ★ Chuck "Pops" Council for sharing letters home and photographs
- ★ Charlie Deppen for sharing letters home, photographs, and writing Your Recovery of August 15
- ★ Maurice Harrington for contributing to the event "The Beach"
- ★ Dennis Stout for sharing photographs and contributing to the event "Working the Red Ball"
- ★ Dusty Rhoades for sharing photographs and contributing to the event "Sappers in the Perimeter" and writing Your Recovery of July 14
- ★ Ryan Okino for contributing to the event "Sappers in the Perimeter"

* John "Mississippi" DeLoach for sharing photographs and for contributing to the event "Ambush"
* Cliff Sivadge for sharing photographs and writing of the events of "Learning of January 14"
* Tommy Thompson for sharing photographs and writing Your Recovery of August 15
* Don Ayres for sharing photographs
* Barry Suda for sharing photographs
* Leslie Pressley for sharing photographs

Thank you to the individuals outside the platoon who contributed:
* Larry Solie for sharing photographs
* Louis Bohn for sharing photographs
* Brenda Jones for sharing photographs
* Bruce Nugget for sharing photographs
* Clint Whitmer for sharing photographs
* Tom Powell for sharing photographs
* Carl Bjelland for sharing photographs
* Steve Tippon, *Southern Cross Newspaper*, for sharing photographs and article

A special thanks to Manny Robinson, John Felchak, Suzanne Potts, Kevin and Jenni Dane, and my wife, Sherrie, for helping me to get the book ready for publication.

INTRODUCTION

I was 18 years old when I graduated from high school in Columbus, Georgia, in July 1968. I had brown hair and a small frame—five feet, seven inches and only 135 pounds. After graduation, I enlisted in the Army Infantry/Airborne for three years. I felt called to serve, and I understood my obligation. I knew Vietnam would be my destination, my first time away from home.

My father was an Army Captain, and my mother a homemaker. My father served with the infantry during World War II. He saw combat in Europe at the Battle of Anzio and served as an Adjutant with the 199th Infantry Brigade in Vietnam in 1967. He retired while I was in Vietnam. I have an older brother, Wayne (his first name is John), who went with me to Vietnam, and a younger sister, Charlene.

I turned 19 on April 15, 1969. I experienced the hardships of a Vietnam tour and the horrors of combat after my 19th birthday. I shared these experiences with the men of my infantry platoon, First Platoon. My brothers.

My story comes from my memories of events that happened 47 years ago. Through its telling, I honor the men of First Platoon and share the experiences we had together. I remember with great sadness the men who never made it home.

While writing this memoir, the events came to me distorted by the stress of war and years gone by—quite possibly not in chronological order. The year 1969 does not play as a continuous slide show of memories in my mind but as a slide show from a jumbled tray of dropped slides. My slides appear out of sequence, with some missing altogether. It was both frustrating and humorous how my memory stored the events and how difficult it was to recall specific instances.

I used Battalion daily journals, maps, military websites, casualty reports, letters home, and platoon member stories to help build a complete account as accurately as possible. I have done my best to describe in detail my year with First Platoon as it happened.

The letters in this book are transcribed from the originals written home and to friends. The platoon members who authored the letters have asked that they remain as written, with no editing, revising, or correcting.

CHAPTER 1

BECOMING SOLDIERS

GROWING UP AS **A**RMY BRATS, we moved many times and had to start over, meeting new people and going to new schools. We lived in Heidelberg, Germany (my birthplace), North Augusta, South Carolina, Fort Monroe, Virginia, Orléans, France, and Columbus, Georgia. My brother Wayne, 16 months older than me, and I were best friends and close during these years. We had our arguments and fights, but we looked out for each other. He was more serious than I and had a temper. I was always joking around, trying to make family and friends laugh, and was more easy going. My mother called me "Jerry Lewis" because of my constant antics.

Wayne repeated third grade, so we were in the same grade and sometimes the same classroom through our school years. He was always bigger than me, and in high school our friends called him "Big Haynie" and me "Little Haynie." Wayne entered the Army at six feet tall, 160 pounds.

I had a normal childhood. I played basketball, baseball, and football after school based on the sports season and was a good athlete playing sandlot sports. I was never big or fast enough to make most high school teams but made the wrestling team my junior year; I didn't try out my senior year. I played tuba in the high school band, though I balked at marching band due to my size versus the tuba's size. Reading was a passion, and I read two books at a time, with a book hidden in the school library and a book at home. There were times I would skip a class and go to the library to read. I was a C student in high school, only because I didn't apply myself. Heck, I had to go to summer school to graduate! Learning that I wouldn't graduate with my class, I decided not to attend the prom or senior class outing. I showed the teacher who failed me!

During my junior high school years and freshman year of high school, bigger kids picked on me because of my size. They walked along the hall between classes and hit me in the stomach, slapped the back of my head, or frogged my arm. A lot of times Wayne stepped in to "save" me. I was tired of being picked on and Wayne stepping in, so during my sophomore year, I picked a fight with one of the biggest kids in school, one of my tormentors. At the beginning of the school year, I walked up to him in the hall and shoved him. Surprised, he asked what I thought I was doing. With my meanest look, I said, "Meet me after school behind the gym." He smiled and said, "You be there." We met, and many of our classmates circled us; I tried not to let my fear show. I tried to give a good fight, landing one lucky punch just under his left eye. I don't think he even noticed. He whipped my ass. No one picked on me after the fight. That one ass whipping was worth it!

My parents were strict, so I thought. They needed to know where we were and enforced an 11:00 pm curfew. I thought 11:00 pm too early, so getting home later was normal for me. Getting grounded was the typical punishment for getting home late. Being grounded didn't bother me because it gave me more time to read. This became a continuous cycle. I became more rebellious as I got older and closer to graduating from high school.

I didn't have a driver's license because my parents said I needed to buy the car and pay for the insurance before getting a license. I could never afford a car and insurance. I had to walk to my girlfriend's house two miles away and had to double date with a friend who had a car. My mother took me for my driver's test right before I left for Vietnam; I passed.

After graduating from high school, I needed to decide my future. My parents expected that once I graduated I would go to college, get a good job, or join the military. Any of the three meant you needed to leave the house and live on your own. I had no money for college—and wasn't ready academically, either—and I had no real job. The decision was easy join the Army. I knew a war was going on and that I would go. Aren't you supposed to serve your country?

I didn't tell Wayne or my parents of my plans to enlist until I'd talked with the recruiter and discussed joining the Army. I wanted this to be my decision. As soon as Wayne learned I'd enlisted, he volunteered for the draft and would leave for active duty one week after me. Our mother and father supported our decision and were proud we volunteered to serve, but we did not talk about the odds of us having to go to war. Our family was not big on communication or expressing emotions. We watched the evening news and saw the body count of American soldiers killed and wounded each week. This was something you could not ignore.

On July 30, 1968, I reported for Basic Combat Training (BCT) at Fort Benning, Georgia. Wayne reported for training the week after I did. I was at the training location known as Sand Hill, and Wayne was at the training location Harmony Church ten miles from me, assigned to separate training brigades providing the same training.

We found BCT had its challenges but was not that difficult. We did physical training and learned of military customs and traditions—US Army ranks, drill and ceremony, first aid, hand-to-hand combat, basic rifle marksmanship with an M-14 rifle, and how to arm and throw a grenade, to name a few requirements. For my outstanding performance,

I received a promotion to Private E2 after graduation. Wayne and I completed BCT and reported to Fort Gordon, Georgia, for Advanced Individual Training (AIT). Our AIT was specialized for infantry airborne trainees. After graduation from AIT, we would go to airborne training at Fort Benning. The training battalion assigned me to Alpha Company and Wayne to Bravo Company. Our company barracks were near each other and provided the same training.

The infantry training was more challenging and difficult than BCT. We were in the field for days at a time to learn ambushes, patrolling techniques, booby traps, and how to sweep a Vietnamese village. The company learned to work as small units and to use fire-and-maneuver techniques to engage an enemy force. We became proficient with different weapons systems: M-16 rifle, M-79 grenade launcher, M-60 machine gun, M-72 light anti-tank weapon (LAW), .45 caliber pistol and a .50 caliber machine gun. During our last week of training, my company flew by helicopter to another army post, Fort Stewart, Georgia, and learned how to perform a combat assault into enemy territory. Upon graduating AIT, I received a promotion to Private First Class E3 for outstanding performance. Wayne and I were ready for a break after our infantry training but thought it had prepared us for Vietnam.

After completion of AIT, we had a 10-day leave for the Christmas season. (Army training stopped a week before Christmas and did not resume until after the New Year.) This Christmas season was like any other. Wayne and I visited friends and spent time with family. We tried to impress our father with our newfound military knowledge. He played along, acting as if our knowledge impressed him. Christmas morning, Wayne and I got a shotgun with a box of ammunition from dad, which was a surprise. We never had guns in the house or were around guns. Wayne and I went to the woods on Fort Benning and spent Christmas, a cold crisp day, shooting at invisible targets and talked about our infantry training and going to airborne school. Our parents never talked about Vietnam or Wayne and me going to war. We did not bring up the topic, either. After the 10 days passed, we reported to Fort Benning for

Airborne School, and the headquarters company clerk assigned us to the same platoon.

Airborne training consisted of three one-week phases: ground week, tower week, and jump week. If you were unlucky, which we were, upon arriving at Airborne School, you received a zero week. Zero week was nothing but working details and Kitchen Police (KP)—what I refer to as "free labor"; it had nothing to do with training. During the second week of training, I got the Hong Kong flu and was bedridden for a week. My instructor told me I needed to repeat the training I had just completed. I decided not to repeat the training and quit Airborne School. Wayne quit, too, so we could stay together.

Wayne and I received orders to Vietnam and were assigned to a 12-month tour; we reported the same day. We went home to begin our 30-day leave before reporting to Fort Lewis, Washington, for processing to Vietnam.

Now that we had orders for Vietnam, the discussion came up with our parents. They both assumed we would go to Vietnam and encouraged us to be careful and take care of each other. What could parents say when their sons are going to war together? Dad did not make many comments or give much advice. The only thing I remember him saying was, "Let your training and instincts guide you." I think mom and dad avoided talking about Vietnam and war because it was easier on them. I explained to them I would try to get Wayne out of going because of the brothers-in-country rule. The Army rule was that brothers not serve in a combat zone at the same time. Once we got to Fort Lewis, I would ask that Wayne stay and I go.

I made sure I watched the evening news every night. The news showed live footage of the fighting and reported higher body counts of American soldiers killed and wounded each week. In 1968, there were 16,899 servicemen killed in Vietnam. This war was not going away. I think the awareness of going to war was finally taking over my thoughts. Nothing would happen to me, but my stomach felt uneasy, with fear creeping inside me.

One evening I was out with a friend, Edwin, driving to another friend's house. The county police observed Edwin driving and pulled us over to the side of the road. Edwin didn't have a valid driver's license. The police searched the car and trunk and found a fishing knife inside a tackle box. The officer proclaimed Edwin had a concealed weapon. I said, "Hell, man, that is not a weapon," and before I knew it, a police officer had slammed me onto the hood of the car, handcuffed me, and arrested me for using profanity.

They locked me up in the city jail overnight, and I went to court the next morning. The judge asked the police officer what happened, and he exaggerated the language I used. The judge, a retired Army officer, said I was a disgrace to the uniform and should never talk to a police officer that way. He gave me the choice of 30 days or a $150.00 fine and sent me back to jail into general population. The inmates had sentences for various types of crimes, including violent crimes. Not my type of people.

I don't know why I used profanity to the police officer; I knew better. I guess I got frustrated by how they'd handled the stop. Or maybe I was afraid of going to war, and I used the traffic stop as my last chance to express my fear. Either way, I knew the right choice. I made my phone call and told Wayne where to find my money. He paid the fine, and I got released that afternoon.

We left the next day, March 9, 1969, for Vietnam, saying our good-byes to our parents and sister at the Columbus, Georgia, airport—no big emotional goodbye, but a brief hug with my mother and sister and a handshake from my dad. We boarded our flight and flew to Fort Lewis, Washington, the first stop on a long journey.

GOING TO VIETNAM

Our flight landed at the Seattle, Washington, airport. After getting off the plane, we got our bags and headed to the United Service Organizations (USO) room at the far end of the airport. From the USO location, we caught a military bus to Fort Lewis. Upon arrival at Fort Lewis, we departed the bus with our gear and reported. Once we reported to the replacement company, I requested to see the Company Commander to ask that Wayne not go to Vietnam. The Army had a policy that brothers not serve in a combat zone together.

We decided that I should go because I had a three-year enlistment, and Wayne had a two-year enlistment. I had time on my enlistment to complete a Vietnam tour after Wayne returned if he went first. Both of us shouldn't do tours in Vietnam.

I asked the Commander, and he stated, "Private, you don't have a brother in-country, so the rule doesn't apply."

I said, "Sir, look at our orders. We are both listed as going to Vietnam."

The commander repeated his statement: "Private, you don't have a brother in-country, so the rule doesn't apply." Army logic, at least in the Vietnam era!

The replacement company issued Wayne and me jungle fatigues and boots. We changed to the jungle fatigues, laced our boots, and packed away our dress uniform and shoes. Wayne and I departed Seattle, Washington, early in the morning on March 10, 1969, for Vietnam for our 12-month tour. We got little sleep before departing.

We boarded an airliner with a flight crew and stewardesses just like any other domestic or international flight. The passengers were servicemen, and the destination Vietnam. The stewardesses made sure they were nice to us during the flight. They understood where we were going. While serving drinks and meals, the stewardesses made friendly conversation with the young men on the flight heading to war. We had stops in Anchorage, Alaska, and then Tokyo, Japan, before arriving at Cam Ranh Bay, South Vietnam, on March 11, 1969.

My first memories of Vietnam are of the heat and the smells. They differed from anything I had ever experienced. The heat was unbearable, as if the sun was closer to the ground in Vietnam than back home. And the stench was a mixture of burning human waste, diesel fuel, jet fuel, strange food, and various human odors. I can still smell that terrible aroma all these years later.

We disembarked the airplane and moved toward a group of buildings. The dark-green painted buildings had a wooden frame and were screened on the top half of the wall on all four sides. The enlisted men moved to an area behind the buildings and lined up in formation. The Non-Commissioned Officer in Charge (NCOIC) conducted a roll call.

He called the name, "Haynie, G."

I said, "Here."

He next called the name, "Haynie, J."

Wayne said, "Here."

The NCOIC asked, "Are you two related?"

Wayne responded, "Yes, we are brothers." No one in authority reacted to our response.

On our first night at Cam Ranh Bay, the reception company First Sergeant assigned us to guard duty. The Sergeant of the Guard (SOG) and a truck driver took us to our guard position with other replacements for guard duty. The driver stopped the truck at a bunker on the perimeter.

The SOG said, "Haynie and Haynie, here is your guard position" as we got off the truck at 2200 hours. Wayne and I headed to the bunker with our M-16s and one magazine of ammunition each.

The SOG stopped us and said, "Lock and load your weapon." First, we checked that the M-16 selector switch was on safe. We inserted the magazine and pulled the charging handle to the rear and released it to load a bullet into the chamber. We moved to the front of the bunker, and the SOG gave further instructions: "I will pick you two up at midnight."

Once we were inside the bunker, the SOG said, "If you see a red flare, that means it's an enemy attack; If it's a green flare, it's all-clear." I got afraid because I didn't know the difference between red and green (I learned two years later I was red/green color blind). It was good that Wayne was with me.

The bunker appeared to be old, held together with wooden beams and covered with several layers of different-colored old, leaking sandbags. The inside smelled of mildew, and the dirt floor was wet. Wayne and I had a good view to our front. We had a cleared field to our front fifty meters wide which ran into heavy vegetation consisting of tall trees, high brush, grass, and bamboo. We could not see past the wall of vegetation. The bunker design had open-slot windows cut into its front. At least it was protection.

We performed our guard duty with no flares going off or enemy attacking our bunker. To be honest, Wayne pulled guard while I slept. I did not take the guard duty seriously, being on one of the biggest military installations in Vietnam; I guess my maturity, or lack of, showed here. The truck picked us up on time, and the change of the guards happened without incident. Arriving at the replacement compound, Wayne and I climbed out the back of the truck. We cleared our weapons and headed to the arms room to turn in our weapons and ammunition. At last, we settled in for some much-needed rest. I slumped over on my bunk and soon fell fast asleep.

The next day, we completed our in-processing and learned of our assignments to the American (23rd Infantry) Division in Chu Lai. Fifty soldiers, including Wayne and I, in a column of twos, loaded onto a C-130 and flew to Chu Lai, the American Division base, for movement to our units. This was where we received orders for our assigned infantry unit within the Division. Once we landed and departed the plane through the rear ramp, we boarded a military bus for transport to the American Division Combat Center. The Combat Center was where replacements reported. Infantry, Armor, Artillery, and Combat Engineer soldiers (Combat Arms) had an in-country six-day training period before going to their units, and other soldiers had a three-day training period. Once we arrived, we departed the bus carrying our gear. We moved to a road, not far from the South China Sea, where the commander held a formation and conducted a roll call.

He called the name, "Haynie, G."

I said, "Here, sir."

He next called the name, "Haynie, J."

Wayne said, "Here, sir."

The commander asked, "Are you two related?"

Wayne responded, "Yes sir, we are brothers."

The company commander of the Combat Center assigned us to his unit until he decided what to do with us. At last, someone had listened. The commander assigned Wayne as a truck driver, and one of his jobs was delivering mail. He assigned me to the supply room. We attended none of the in-country training. While serving as a supply clerk at the Combat Center, one of my assignments was to accept, log, and store duffle bags and other gear for soldiers leaving the country for leave or other purposes.

One day in late March, a young soldier with brown hair, standing five feet, eight inches tall and weighing 145 pounds, walked into the supply room carrying a duffle bag and other gear. At first glance, I noticed that he looked sad and distracted, so I assumed it was combat related.

We greeted each other, and I asked, "How can I help you?"

He stated he was going back to the states for emergency leave and needed to store his gear. I told him "No problem. I will handle it."

I asked, "What is your name so I can fill out the log and tag your gear?"

He responded, "Michael Dankert."

I asked, "Where are you from?"

"Wayne, Michigan," he replied.

Once I tagged and stored his gear, Dankert left the supply room and got in a jeep. The driver drove along the dirt road toward the airfield. I didn't think of this meeting until much later. Mike Dankert and I would ultimately get assigned to the same platoon. I arrived to the platoon first, and after he returned from leave, Mike received his assignment to the platoon.

Wayne and I continued to learn and do our jobs while they were deciding what to do with us. My job as the supply clerk consisted of receiving luggage and gear from departing soldiers, logging it, and storing it in the proper location to make sure it would be easily found. The supply sergeant told me to rearrange the stored gear; this was boring and tedious work. Once I moved something to a new location, I changed the log to show the new location. Paperwork!

Wayne learned the route and mailroom locations to deliver and pick up mail from different units. In the morning, he went to the division mailroom to pick up the units' mail, delivered the mail, and picked up outgoing mail to take back to the division mailroom. He had many other tasks that involved using the truck to pick up soldiers or equipment to be shuttled. He got the better job.

ROCKET ATTACK

Wayne and I were lying on our bunks getting ready for lights out. The shriek of a siren warning us of a rocket attack made us jump out of our bunks—our first rocket attack. We looked at each other, with no idea what to do. Wayne yelled, "Run for the bunker!" We grabbed our M-16s, put on our helmets and boots, and busted out the front door, turning left to run to our assigned bunker. With helmets on, weapons in hand, wearing only our underclothes (olive-green boxer shorts and t-shirts) and combat boots, we crawled into the dark bunker as we heard explosions continue from the distance. The bunker was nothing more than a corrugated metal pipe five feet in diameter and ten feet long. Three layers of sandbags covered the pipe. As we sat there waiting for the all-clear siren, I worried about the rats living in the bunker. Supposedly, Vietnam rats were as big as cats.

We heard several more loud explosions in the distance. After 15 minutes, we received the all-clear signal. Wayne and I crawled back out of the bunker and headed to our hooch. We'd survived our first enemy attack and thought we'd been baptized under fire. We received a couple more rocket attacks over the coming weeks and repeated the same drill to get to the bunker.

OUTDOOR MOVIE

One evening the outdoor theater was showing *The Green Berets*, starring John Wayne. Our roommate, Wayne, and I decided to watch the movie. They asked me to pick up a case of beer and meet them at the theater. At 1900 hours, I had the beer and headed to the 1930 hours showing of the movie. Wayne and our roommate never showed. I sat there drinking beer after beer while watching the movie. I didn't even like or drink beer. Before I knew it, I was drunk—I mean zig-zag walking, mumbling, stumbling drunk.

I got to our hooch, fell into my bunk, and puked on myself, the floor, and my bed. Wayne woke up, and he was angry that I'd woken him with my drunken behavior. He grabbed me and tossed me outside into the sand in front of our hooch. I felt nothing. I lay there in the sand, unable to stand. Our roommate told Wayne not to leave me lying outside but to get me showered. After 10 minutes of arguing with our roommate, Wayne agreed and took me to the showers.

I stripped off my puke-covered uniform and underclothes. Wayne held me up under the shower head while the cold water washed the puke off of me. Once I was clean, I moved away from the shower head and thought, *Shit, I don't have clean clothes!*

Off to my right was a soldier showering, and he had clean, folded underclothes on the bench. I walked toward the soldier and, while looking this large, six feet, two inch, 200-pound man right in the eye, picked up his underclothes and put them on my skinny body. We walked out of the shower room with no one saying a word and headed back to our hooch. I'm sure I was a sight wearing this soldier's underclothes, because of my small size. I am surprised that the soldier didn't rip my head off my shoulders.

It was the end of April, and Wayne and I had many discussions on who would stay or leave Vietnam. I had a three-year enlistment, and Wayne had a two-year enlistment. It only made sense that I stay. If Wayne stayed for a one-year tour, I still had two years left on my enlistment and more than likely would get orders for Vietnam. If I stayed, Wayne wouldn't have enough time on his two-year enlistment to return to Vietnam. Wayne thought he should stay because he was the older brother but finally agreed and accepted the Company Commander's recommendation to go to Korea.

The night of April 30, 1969, Wayne and I said our goodbyes, and we acknowledged this would be the first time we'd be separated from each other. The morning of May 1, 1969, Wayne left for Korea, and I departed for my new assignment to Company A 3/1 of the 11th Brigade. I was on my own.

Figure 1. Glyn and Wayne Haynie outside our home going to Vietnam March 1969. Photo provided by Glyn Haynie.

Figure 3. Combat Center outdoor theater where Glyn Haynie saw *The Green Berets*. Photo provided by Clint Whitmer.

Figure 2. Americal Division Combat Center, from where we left for our units. The shipping shed is on the right. Photo provided by Clint Whitmer.

CHAPTER 3

THE LONG JOURNEY BEGINS

I received orders to the 11th Brigade 3/1Bn Company A two weeks after my 19th birthday. The company driver and jeep arrived early morning at my hooch to take me to the airport. We arrived, and I got out of the jeep, thanked the driver, and walked to the desk for departures. I showed my orders, and the NCOIC said my flight would leave in 30 minutes. I took a seat and waited. In a short time, the NOCIC called my flight for boarding. I walked along the tarmac with other soldiers and approached the C-130, using the open rear door as a ramp. I found a seat near the front. Once everyone was on board, the rear door closed. There was equipment, supplies, and 10 soldiers on board the airplane. The C-130 taxied along the runway, gathering speed until it lifted into the air. It was early morning, and I was flying to a Fire Support Base (FSB) named Bronco at Duc Pho, located 90 miles south of Da Nang. After the plane landed, I got a ride by jeep from the landing strip to the Alpha Company headquarters.

The company First Sergeant, First Sergeant Malpica, smoking a large, smelly cigar, greeted and briefed me on the company and its current location and mission. The First Sergeant was a career soldier in his mid-thirties, with dark hair and medium build. He sent me to supply to store my luggage and receive my combat issue of equipment, including helmet with liner (worn under the helmet for fit and comfort), rucksack, poncho, poncho liner, three canteens, first aid pouches with bandages, three days of rations, and M-16 rifle with ammunition.

The supply clerk instructed me on what personal items I should take. The items included stationery and pen, toothbrush and paste, toilet paper, razor, soap, mosquito repellent, cigarettes, lighter with flint and fluid, Bible, and camera with film. The clerk even showed me the best way to get everything packed while distributing the weight into the rucksack. As he helped pack the rucksack with personal and field items, he explained how supplies reached me in the field. He then issued a claymore mine, two trip flares, one pound of C-4, two regular hand grenades, and one smoke grenade. He showed me how to pack these items. I asked about the C-4, stating that I wasn't an engineer and didn't know how to blow things up. He said I would use the C-4 to heat my rations. It turned out he was an infantry veteran working as a supply clerk as his rear job before returning home the following month. He was informative and helpful.

After I received my gear, I reported back to the First Sergeant. He checked me out and then pointed at a large, dirty truck with canvas covering the back.

He said, "Haynie, get on that truck; it will take you to the company at FSB Charlie Brown. Once there, report to Captain Tyson."

"Yes, First Sergeant," I replied.

As I moved toward the truck, I thought about how heavy my rucksack felt! I threw my rucksack (well, maybe *pushed* it onto the back of the truck) and then climbed up and over the tailgate. There was an empty seat near the back opening next to several soldiers. They appeared to be a mixture of replacements and veterans. The bright-green uniforms and looks of awe were a giveaway in identifying the replacements. The veterans had old, faded uniforms, scuffed dirty boots, stubble growth on their faces, and longer hair. They looked at you with piercing but sad eyes.

A sergeant came to the back of the truck and said, "I will tell you when we reach Ambush Alley. And you need to be alert; we may need your help."

Ambush Alley was a location along Highway 1 where the enemy attacked exposed convoys. The location gave the enemy cover and concealment, providing the perfect location for an ambush.

I made eye contact with the replacement sitting across from me. He looked 16 years old, with red hair. And he had a nervous smile on his freckled face. We looked at each other in disbelief that they needed our help. That statement had made me nervous. Once the sergeant climbed into the front passenger seat, the truck jerked forward, with its gears grinding, to join the convoy of jeeps and several more trucks heading south to the firebase.

The soldiers I rode with were quiet; no one said a word. After 30 minutes on the road, the sergeant in the front seat yelled over the roar of the truck engine that we were going through Ambush Alley and for us to be alert. The veterans appeared to become even more tense. I mentally prepared myself to engage the enemy if needed. I didn't know what else to do. As we rolled along, I looked out the back of the truck at the strange countryside. During the trip we passed rice paddies, hills, mountains, heavy jungle growth, and villagers with their water buffalo working in the rice paddies or walking along the highway. On the other side of the highway a beach with the glare of white sand against the blue water of the South China Sea came into view. I thought, *What a contrast between the two sides of the highway.* The one-hour ride was uneventful.

The truck drove as far as it could before reaching the South China Sea. We boarded a Navy landing craft that ferried us to a small island surrounded by the South China Sea. We arrived at FSB Charlie Brown. I reported to the Company Commander (CO), Captain Tyson. He had a weathered face and looked older than the average captain, with short brown hair and about five feet, ten inches, weighing 155 pounds. He was a rugged-looking officer.

Captain Tyson assigned me to First Platoon (see Appendix A) and told me I would leave in two hours. He stated the platoon leader, Lieutenant Baxter, was a good officer, and he led a good platoon of soldiers. I learned later that Captain Tyson had been in the Special Forces as an enlisted medic before he went to Officer Candidate School (OCS), was knowledgeable, and spoke Vietnamese. Captain Tyson, assigned to the company in March 1969, had the respect and trust of the soldiers of Alpha Company. His endorsement of Lieutenant Baxter proved right.

Captain Tyson gave a quick briefing on the company and battalion. He said the company had three infantry platoons (First Platoon, Second Platoon, and Third Platoon) and one Weapons Platoon with 81mm and 60mm mortars. He said that each platoon had between 25 and 30 soldiers assigned. The Battalion Commander, Lieutenant Colonel George Ellis, assigned to the battalion in April 1969, had combat experience and had been a Non-Commissioned Officer (NCO) before he completed Army Reserve Officers' Training Corps (ROTC) in college. The battalion had six companies. Four of the companies were infantry companies—Alpha, Bravo, Charlie, and Delta. The fifth company, Echo Company, was comprised of the Recon Platoon, 4.2inch mortars, and platoons responsible for minesweeping and demolition. The last company was the Headquarters and Headquarters Company, which included the service and support soldiers, medics, cooks, clerks, supply, and battalion staff. After the briefing, Captain Tyson told me to wait outside for the helicopter. I saluted and moved outside the command bunker.

It wasn't long as I sat on the ground outside the command bunker waiting until a clerk stuck his head out the bunker entrance and told me to head to the helicopter pad to catch my flight. I grabbed my weapon and gear and headed to the pad. Once the Huey landed, I boarded and sat on the floor (no seats on the helicopters we flew on), with my weapon pointed downward, safety on and no bullet in the chamber, as taught.

This eliminated the odds of a bullet accidentally being discharged and hitting the engine or rotor. This was standard practice for flying on any helicopter. The Huey slowly lifted into the air and then accelerated, banking hard right with the distinctive "whoop, whoop, whoop" sound of the blades cutting through the air as we departed for the platoon location.

As the helicopter descended after 20 minutes in flight, I looked down on the rugged terrain and jungle growth. I spotted a small field covered with tall elephant grass and watched the grass flatten from rotor wash as the helicopter descended and landed. As I jumped off, with no idea what to expect, a menacing-looking soldier with red hair and beard darted out of the jungle growth, ran toward me, and yelled, "Follow me." This was my introduction to Bruce Tufts. Charlie Deppen, a platoon member, later told me that Bruce Tufts reminded him of a Viking; I thought that an excellent description. In civilian life, Bruce was a schoolteacher from New Jersey. At 26 years old, he was older than most of us.

Tufts introduced me to the command post group (CP): Lieutenant John Baxter, our Platoon Leader, Leslie Pressley, the lieutenant's Radio Telephone Operator (RTO), Doc Windows (see Appendix B), the Platoon Medic, Terry Daron, the Platoon Sergeant's RTO, and Sergeant Plummer, the Platoon Sergeant. Lieutenant Baxter was 26 years old, tall, and clean cut. He presented himself as a professional Army officer. I was at once impressed. He assigned me to the first squad, and he introduced the Squad Leader, Sergeant Michael Stout (see Appendix C). I found it ironic, because his brother, Dennis, was also in the squad.

Sergeant Stout was from Iowa. He was muscular, had receding light-brown hair, and wore glasses. He was only 19 years old, but he had experience and was the younger brother, several years younger than Dennis. He introduced me to the squad: Juan Ramos, Maurice Harrington, Dennis Stout, Tim "Dusty" Rhoades, Joe Mitchell, Warren McVey, Amby Sanchez, and Jack Lanzer.

After the quick introductions, Sergeant Stout stated that I would go on Observation Post (OP) duty (Heck—I've been here ten minutes!), and I followed him through the thick elephant grass to a position where

Paul Ponce was on OP duty for the platoon. The position was on a ridge that overlooked a large valley with two hills on each side of the ridge covered in dense jungle growth. The elephant grass was up to my shoulders. He introduced me to Paul. We nodded at each other. Paul was from California, married, short, with black hair. He was 20 years old and had a quick smile.

Sergeant Stout handed me a grenade, and, while I was holding it, he pulled the pin. As he and Ponce were leaving, he said, "I will be back in an hour." I had a tight grasp on the grenade, holding the handle so it would not release. I held it so tightly my hand lost color. If I'd released the handle, the grenade would have exploded in four or five seconds.

I later learned that the term "OP" was a position for early warning of an enemy attack or movement during the day and that Listening Post (LP) was a position for early warning during the night. The OP and LP positions are forward of the squad and platoon positions. I was alone and charged with warning the platoon if I saw any Viet Cong (VC) or North Vietnamese Army soldiers (NVA).

He returned in an hour and, without saying a word, replaced the pin. I don't know if the grenade had a blasting cap or was a dud, but I treated it as if it could explode. I guess I passed the test. I followed him back to the platoon position. While walking back, I kept flexing my hand to regain mobility.

It amazed me the platoon was half the size it should be. A typical infantry platoon had 4 squads and 44 members. Our platoon had 25 members divided into two squads, with 10 soldiers each and 5 with the command post (CP): the Platoon Leader, Platoon Sergeant, RTO for the Platoon Leader and Platoon Sergeant, and the Platoon Medic. Each squad had an M-60 machine gunner, assistant gunner, and an M-79 grenade launcher. The rest of the soldiers were riflemen with M-16s.

We patrolled our Area of Operation (AO) as a platoon, separate from the other platoons in the company. That night, as I sat in my position pulling my two-hour guard shift, I thought of the events of my first day. I realized that, in one day, I had flown on a C-130 personnel/transport plane to get to Duc Pho, had ridden in a 2 1/2-ton truck, and had boarded a landing craft to be ferried to FSB Charlie Brown; then I'd flown in a Huey to be dropped off at my platoon location in the jungle. I'd used many modes of transportation to get to my new "home."

Here I am, 10 months out of high school, with a rifle and ammunition, grenades, rocket launcher, and mines. I was trusted to use any of these weapons to kill. I glanced behind me at the squad, sound asleep, wrapped in their poncho liners, trusting me with their lives. And here I sat in the jungle with these strangers and no clue what I was doing!

The next day we started humping early, walking with our gear, ammunition, and weapons through the hot and humid jungle. I was sweating heavily and drank water until my canteens were empty. My 50-pound rucksack was getting heavier by the hour. After hours of walking, I saw the sky darken and my surroundings spin before I crumbled to the ground, unconscious from the heat. I came to with squad members loosening my clothes and dousing me with water to cool me. I thought, *What a way to start off with a new unit*. I felt terrible that they had to waste their water.

I heard someone say, "FNG down!" Now I'm even more embarrassed.

Then the same rugged red-haired soldier from second squad stopped and said, "Don't worry, Haynie; this happens to everyone" and then smiled as he continued to walk past me. I sure felt better.

Lieutenant Baxter had the platoon take a break and said to move out in 30 minutes. I appreciated the time to recover. As I sat leaning against a tree, a shadow fell over me, and I looked up to see Lieutenant Baxter standing over me.

He asked, "How are you doing, Haynie?" I heard the empathy in his voice, and I knew this Lieutenant cared about the soldiers in his platoon and was not pissed or impatient with me for passing out from the heat.

With newfound energy, I replied, "Doing better, Sir."

Lieutenant Baxter continued "Hang in there; we will be back at a firebase in a week." Now I have an incentive to keep moving!

FNG

FNG or "Fucking New Guy" was a label given to new replacements because an FNG was dangerous; he could get you killed. The veterans shunned an FNG. The "Fucking" part of the label was derogatory and meant to be. So it became the goal of each FNG to lose the "F" in the label first. An FNG needed to prove himself to his squad and platoon members.

The FNG needed to carry his weight, listen, and learn. He couldn't be a know-it-all. His accomplishments in the "world" weren't important; they did not matter in Vietnam. No one cared if the Army drafted you, you went to college, or were a high school star quarterback. This was Vietnam! You had to be trusted to pull your OP, LP, and guard duty with no one worrying if you were inattentive or asleep. Their lives depended on you being alert and awake.

An FNG needed to learn basic skills to survive: humping, staying hydrated, avoiding punji sticks and booby traps, walking point, weapon maintenance, hygiene in the field, and using C-4 to cook C-rations or heat water. He needed to learn that the platoon didn't tolerate drug use. Once you achieved the basics, the "F" part of the label dropped off, and the veterans referred to you as the "New Guy," until a new replacement reported to the squad. Then the cycle began again.

We took a required malaria pill daily and a second pill weekly without supervision. The weekly pill was a large orange pill and caused diarrhea for two or three days. With these side effects, some platoon members skipped taking this pill. We used diethyltoluamide (DEET), which was a mosquito repellent issued in a two-ounce plastic bottle to ward off mosquitos before they bit you. We applied DEET several times a day to any exposed skin because your sweat or rain would wash the protection away. Malaria was another enemy we learned to avoid. If we caught malaria, we went to the rear for medical attention.

We made sure we drank plenty of water to avoid being a heat casualty. Clean water wasn't always available, so we used iodine tablets to purify the water. Iodine tablets gave the water a nasty taste. We had to get water from wells, rivers, and streams. If we didn't purify the water, we might get sick and have to be sent to the rear for medical attention.

We had to make sure we treated our jungle rot. Jungle rot was a sore or lesion that developed every time you got a cut anywhere on the body, normally arms and legs, from the elephant grass or thorns in the jungle growth. Not being able to bathe and change clothes regularly and exposure to heat, humidity, water, and wet clothing made it worse. The sore appeared in the size of a nickel to a quarter. The sore oozed pus and blood, itched, and hurt. It might be so infected we needed to go to the brigade hospital for treatment.

Basic Training and AIT taught us how and how often to clean and keep your weapon. But in Vietnam, it was crucial to keep your weapon maintained at all times. Vietnam was wet, hot, and humid. The M-16 had a reputation for jamming and not working. If we didn't clean our weapon regularly, the selector switch could freeze in the safe position, or a bullet could jam in the chamber, or a magazine might not hold the bullets properly to be fed into the chamber. During a firefight, your weapon must work, or you and, worst case, one of your platoon members would get killed or wounded.

It didn't matter how popular drug use was in the world. A soldier using drugs in the field couldn't stay alert, fight, or be trusted. The lives of all platoon members depended on each other, and being on drugs could get a platoon member killed. If a soldier used drugs in the field, he could get injured, get someone killed, or get a court-martial and go to the stockade.

Staying alive and basic survival became the biggest job, not because of the enemy but because the physical exertion was so demanding. An FNG learned to hump in the heat carrying a 60-pound pack and weapon while walking through difficult terrain and always looking for the enemy, booby traps, or ambushes. Once you earned the respect of the veterans, they would teach you everything you needed to know to survive and protect you from harm. Your squad and platoon would become your family. You were no longer the new guy. You were a brother!

FIRE SUPPORT BASE CHARLIE BROWN

We were in the field for a week before the platoon went to Charlie Brown. Companies rotated on and off the firebase every couple of weeks or month. The South China Sea surrounding the FSB gave me a sense of security. Inland villages across the water, with villagers going on with their daily routines, were visible from our positions. There were always fishing boats passing by the island. We hoped they were fishing boats!

We used fortified positions with a bunker shell and wooden beams covered with several layers of sandbags. There we pulled guard, ate, slept, and talked. We swam in the South China Sea, a good break from the boredom. Being on Charlie Brown gave me the opportunity to get to know my platoon members better; we had more time to relax.

My first experience being on a firebase wasn't a good one, although we had hot meals, showers, and outhouses. Someone had to keep everything clean. I remember being on detail every day because I was the FNG. The FNGs had to pull KP, shit burning, and police call (picking up trash) details.

Pulling KP, we assisted the cooks in any task they wanted us to do in the kitchen that didn't involve cooking; this included cleaning trays, cooking utensils, flatware, and the tables where we sat and ate. We served the soldiers moving through the line, and we cleaned up after them as they finished their meals.

Shit-burning detail had to be the worst. A shitter was a row of toilet seats, and under each seat a 55-gallon drum cut in half was used to catch human waste and paper products. The soldiers on detail, working in pairs, slid the full drum out and moved it away from the shitters, poured diesel fuel into the drum, and then lit it on fire. After most of the waste burned off and the drum cooled, we slid it back under the toilet seat. The distinctive smell—human waste and diesel fuel—of the burning drum lingered for years after I returned home.

Police call was the easiest. We walked around with a sandbag and picked up trash around the firebase common areas, mess hall, shitters, showers, and command headquarters. I thought, *I sure hope this is not a combat soldier's life, as it's getting old fast.* Little did I know.

During our stay, Captain Tyson assigned the platoon to guard a bridge right off the firebase on Highway 1—Bridge 58, located south of FSB Charlie Brown and the village of Sa Huynh. Not a large bridge, it covered a river that fed into the sea. As its name suggests, Highway 1 was a main route running north and south along the east coast of Vietnam.

Each day it had heavy traffic that included troop and supply transports and heavy civilian traffic, too. The platoon's job was to secure the bridge and make sure the enemy didn't blow it up or booby trap it. Sandbagged positions were on the north and south side of the bridge, facing away from the ocean and toward the fields and mountains.

Second squad manned the south side, and first squad manned the north side. Only the squad members on guard stayed in the sandbagged positions, while the rest were at the bottom of the bridge, using the bridge and terrain for cover and concealment.

While guarding the bridge, an FNG joined the platoon by the name of Mike Dankert. I didn't recognize him as the soldier I'd met in the supply room at the Combat Center. Lieutenant Baxter assigned Mike to second squad, and the squads interacted little.

I remember the bridge was close to a small Buddhist village near the South China Sea. You could hear sounds of chanting and bells ringing during the day and night, which sounded strange. We tried to concentrate and protect the bridge from the enemy, but the sounds were a distraction. One evening Lieutenant Baxter briefed the platoon of a possible attack and told us we needed to stay vigilant. It was surreal as we lay there waiting for the enemy, with odd sounds and foreign music playing. I commented that it felt like something in the movies. Juan Ramos, from Texas, my height but with more weight, dark hair, and 21 years old, reminded me that this was "not the movies but real life."

This is an excerpt from a letter Lieutenant John Baxter wrote to his parents May 7, 1969.

Greetings from Bridge 58 just south of LZ Charlie Brown & the village of Sa Huynh. We came in from the field to LZ CB yesterday

after a dusty 10 km ride on Armored Personnel Carriers. My platoon—now down to 18—is guarding 2 bridges on either side of LZ Charlie Brown. They are major bridges on HWY#1 i.e. "The Red Ball". . . nice thing is hot chow—3 times a day—instead of once a week and the river is swimmable . . . This am I went with C.O. to meet the village chief and local military authorities. Vaguely reminded me of meetings with Chileans but my Vietnamese is up to 15 words—So that is one big difference M-16's another.

The bridge is by a small Buddhist village about 100 meters from S.China Sea. They pray, chant and ring bells all night really weird when you're trying to keep people from coming through the wire.

One thing about my platoon I don't think I've mentioned. I have 2 brothers in one squad-a real rarity but they wanted to be together-they're from Iowa. My RTO is a country boy from Greenville, So.Carolina. My platoon sergeant is an E-5 from Lexington, NC and his RTO is from Manitowoc, Wisc.

Days later Captain Tyson assigned the platoon to send a patrol to the foothills north of the bridge. He suspected enemy movement in the foothills, and the company wanted to get intelligence of what enemy was near our positions or could attack the bridge.

Lieutenant Baxter told the platoon sergeant, Sergeant Plummer, to select second squad members to prepare for the patrol. My squad, first squad, and what remained of the second squad stayed on the bridge with Lieutenant Baxter for security. The patrol consisted of the platoon sergeant, Sergeant Plummer, his RTO Terry Daron, the second squad leader, Jerry Ofstedahl, and five squad members of second squad. I noticed the new guy, Mike Dankert, was with the patrol, too.

The patrol moved out in a staggered column formation heading north toward the foothills. After an hour or more of humping, the patrol reached the foothills, and the point man had the patrol halt. Sergeant Plummer moved forward to see why the patrol had stopped. He spotted 17 North Vietnamese Army (NVA) soldiers moving along a trail only

100 meters from them. Sergeant Plummer signaled for the patrol to get down. He allowed the NVA patrol to move through without firing on them. Once the NVA moved through and Sergeant Plummer thought it was safe, the patrol moved back to the platoon location.

Sergeant Plummer briefed Lieutenant Baxter on what he saw and explained why he didn't fire on the enemy. It was my understanding that Sergeant Plummer got a rear job soon afterwards because of his decision not to fire. It was the rumor that spread through the platoon. We felt that Sergeant Plummer was a good Platoon Sergeant and took the safety of his men seriously. We would go several weeks without a replacement Platoon Sergeant.

This is an excerpt from a letter Lieutenant John Baxter wrote to his parents May 18, 1969, about the mission that day.

> Well, it's the day before Ho Chi Minh's birthday and things have quieted a bit. The platoon is back on bridge guard for a few days. Yesterday we had lot of excitement. The night before I called a fire mission i.e. mortars on an enemy mortar position (about a mile from here). The next morning the C.O. had me send a patrol out. I sent 7 men about 600 meters from here they spotted 17 NVA with wpns on the move. My people stayed concealed & were never spotted as I tried to call mortars on the NVA. But higher command held up clearance & they got away. The bad thing was we think the (NVA) were the same group who shelled a village near here & killed a bunch of civilians. This is the sad part of this whole dirty mess. The innocent Vietnamese who often get clobbered from both sides. Well, so much for my ramblings about the war. I don't mean to scare you about what I see. I just want to tell it like I see it from ground level.

THE BEACH

We were heading back to the field for three weeks, no longer on a fire support base or guarding the bridge, heading south and then west from Charlie Brown. It was hotter, with the temperature more than

100 degrees and not much cooler in the shade. Heat continued to be our enemy.

The night before we left the bridge, we had a sapper attack (NVA or VC, with explosives) who tried to get to our positions. The platoon kept them from reaching us and had no casualties. We got little sleep that night. We lost five men before moving out, two with malaria, two with injuries, and one to a rear job. Now the platoon strength was at its lowest level in months.

The platoon moved south, following along the South China Sea beach, but staying in the vegetation. As usual, we looked for the NVA or VC to make contact. The breeze from the ocean made the heat more bearable. We walked spread out in a staggered column formation, moving through the vegetation. The lead squad, second squad, received enemy fire. The platoon at once halted and sought cover. A distinctive crack of M-16s firing caught my attention. I heard AK-47s firing in return. The two weapons sounded different. Someone yelled that two VC were running along the beach. Lieutenant Baxter moved the platoon forward to engage the enemy, but they fled once the platoon moved closer to their location.

Lieutenant Baxter decided that this was a good location to set up our night logger positions. A "logger" was a temporary defensive perimeter set up by a unit. The terrain was flat but with heavy jungle growth, which bordered the whitest sand we could ever imagine. Not far off, outside the jungle edge, were several graves. I thought it an odd location to bury people.

Sergeant Stout told us to set up our claymores and trip flares. A claymore mine stood on short legs we pushed into the ground, with the front facing the enemy. The mine had "Front" and "Back" written on it to make sure it was positioned correctly. It fired by pressing a trigger device (clicker) connected to the mine by 100 feet of electrical cord, setting off a blasting cap and C-4 inside the mine. This caused the mine to explode, sending hundreds of steel balls 100 meters toward the enemy. A trip flare was a metal container, similar to a grenade, set off by the enemy walking into a wire tied from the flare's safety pin to another object. We placed the flare where a suspected enemy soldier might approach our position. If the enemy "tripped" the wire enough, the safety pin pulled out, setting the flare off, illuminating the enemy's approach. As we set out our claymore mines and trip flares, we could hear small waves hitting the beach. It was relaxing.

As we finished our dinner meal, the conversation started with small talk. Jack Lanzer looked at Maurice Harrington and said, "Hey, Maurice—tell the squad how you got the big scar on your nose."

Maurice was from North Carolina, 20 years old, not much taller than me but not as skinny. He had a good sense of humor. He was the only platoon member called by his first name; we called everyone else by a nickname or last name. I'd never heard his story, so I became interested. Maurice was hesitant to tell the story, but, after prodding and joking from us, he agreed.

Maurice began his story: "It was December 1968, and a pleasant morning, same as any other. The platoon was preparing breakfast and getting ready for the day. I was eating my C-rations. The medic approached the squad, removed his backpack, and dropped it to the ground. He sat next to his gear, retrieved his cleaning kit, and prepared to clean his M-16. He started to disassemble the weapon to give it a good cleaning. At that point, the rifle discharged a bullet. First squad hit the ground, hearing the M-16 being fired and not knowing what had occurred. A bullet pierced the end of my nose and traveled to the soldier sitting next to me, hitting him in the throat. This startled the medic, and he stared at me without moving to help. Several squad members provided first aid to me and the wounded soldier to stop the bleeding. The platoon leader called in for a dust-off. The platoon secured the perimeter, and the squad leader popped smoke to guide the approaching dust-off to our location. Once on the ground, several platoon members loaded me and the wounded soldier on the helicopter, and the helicopter made a rapid takeoff, heading to the Division hospital in Chu Lai. In flight, the crew worked on the wounded soldier, but he died before we could get to the hospital. Later the hospital sent me to Japan for treatment to repair my nose, and after several months they sent me back to the platoon. So here I am."

The story that Maurice told, being accidentally shot by a fellow soldier and with another soldier dying by the same bullet, astonished me. I understood his reluctance to tell the story. It had to frighten Maurice to be shot by a fellow soldier. I decided not to take it for granted that anyone carrying a weapon would handle it safely.

The conversation moved back to chit-chat and "the world." We referred to back home or stateside as "the world." As darkness crept in, the first person on guard duty moved to his guard position, and the rest of the squad wrapped up in their poncho liners, ready for needed sleep.

Not long after I fell asleep, I heard what sounded like a train going through the jungle. Startled, I sat up and grabbed my M-79, ready for a fight. Then I heard the train again and looked upward. I figured out that it was coming from overhead—a battleship out at sea firing support for another unit further inland. More rounds came over our position, and as each round passed, it sounded as if a freight train was overhead. We were glad we were not on the receiving end of those rounds!

This is an excerpt from a letter Lieutenant John Baxter wrote to his parents May 22.

> We're back in the field for about 17 days. We're heading generally west from Charlie Brown . . . It's a lot hotter now than the last time we were out. Must be 95 to 105 in shade and hotter in the sun. The heat has really been tough on a lot of us. I have been able to stand it so far . . . Had a rough night on the bridge before we came out. A Zapper squad suicide squad tried to hit us but they only got to the first of 3 fences of wire. No casualties but we were up all night . . . We have had a rash of illnesses lately so have lost 5 men—2 with malaria. So my operating strength is at its lowest level.

WORKING THE RED BALL (HIGHWAY 1)

It was late May, and we moved from Charlie Brown, the bridges, and beach to an AO west. Our mission was to patrol and protect the Red Ball, frequented by convoys and the VC. It was hot and difficult to breathe as we moved through the rice paddies and villages during the day, climbing to the high ground before nightfall, exhausted before the sunset. I'd become acclimated by then and could tolerate the heat better, but hot was hot. Most afternoons, there were heavy rains for 30 minutes to an hour that soaked us; my uniform and rucksack would weigh an extra two pounds. It took the rest of the afternoon for us to dry out.

There were two high points on opposite sides of the highway that we used to set up for the night. Sometimes we stayed on the high ground during the day and maintained surveillance of the highway. One night we were on the east side of the highway, 50 feet lower than the high point of the west side of the highway. We set up our perimeter as a circle, with each squad position having a field of fire to the front. The platoon command post (CP) was in the middle.

We used the terrain for cover and concealment. Seldom did we dig foxholes or have any structures for protection. At 2300 hours, Sergeant Stout came around, waking each squad member to tell us there might be an attack that night. Those of us not on guard duty tried to stay alert but drifted in and out of sleep. The bright sun appeared over the horizon spilling sunlight over our positions. It had been a long night. With the darkness gone, we felt safer, and the attack didn't happen.

I had pound cake, hot chocolate, and peaches for breakfast. To heat the water, I tore off a chunk of C-4, placed it in an empty can (stove), and then lit the C-4; it burned perfectly to heat the water in my canteen cup for my hot chocolate. We ate our morning rations and then moved downward to the valley below to patrol along the highway.

As we walked along the highway, Coke girls appeared selling their wares, including ice-cold Coke sitting in dirty ice. What a treat to have an ice-cold Coke! The morning hours passed, and we stopped for lunch.

Chicken and noodles, fruit cocktail, and peanut butter and jelly cracker crunch with Kool-Aid was my typical lunch meal.

The platoon continued to move through the paddies, looking for any signs of the VC. We moved through the afternoon rainstorm and climbed to the high point on the west side of the highway to set up for the night. We established our guard roster and perimeter, and then it was dinner time—beef with spice sauce, pears, pound cake and peanut butter and jelly cracker crunch with Kool-Aid. After the meal, we talked about girls, sports, cars, and "the world" for a while and fell asleep as soon as darkness approached.

At 0130 hours, we heard small-arms fire and explosions; we saw many muzzle flashes and the light of the explosions on the high point on the east side of the highway. Enemy soldiers were hitting Bravo Company hard on the hilltop—our location the previous night. The firefight stopped after an hour, and we heard and saw the dust-off helicopters landing and leaving Bravo Company's location.

The next day, we moved in a single file downward from the hilltop to the paddies at the bottom of the hill. We crossed the paddies and Red Ball in a staggered column formation. Moving back into a single-file formation, we climbed to the hilltop on the east side of the highway and arrived at the firefight location. There were signs of the battle, with bloodstains in the soil of their positions, and bandage wrappers and blood-soaked bandages littering the ground. I thought, *This could have been us.* I bet the rest of the platoon did, too.

We moved higher and 200 meters away from where Bravo Company had been. We set up our positions to watch the Red Ball. After lunch, Sergeant Stout said we were going to logger at this location and to set up our nighttime defenses. "Logger" meant putting out trip flares and claymore mines to waylay any approaching enemy.

This gave us the opportunity to see the platoon medic, Doc Windows, to get our jungle rot or any other injury treated. I had jungle rot on my arms and legs, so Doc cleaned each of my sores and wrapped a bandage around my arms and legs to cover the sores. The only way jungle rot healed was to keep it dry and clean. This proved difficult in the field. I didn't like the white bandages on my arms. I thought I could be detected easier and it would give away my position. Once the sore healed, it left a round scar. I still have scars today.

The sun dropped behind the horizon, and the darkness crept toward us. I had two one-hour guard shifts during the night. My last one-hour shift was the last of the night, so I sat and watched the sunrise. I woke the squad members, and we ate breakfast and then retrieved our trip flares and claymore mines. Sergeant Stout gave the order to "saddle up" (get your gear on) and prepare to move out toward the Red Ball. The term "saddle up" came from the television show *Combat*.

The climb downward from the steep hill was difficult but uneventful. Once we reached the bottom, Lieutenant Baxter received a radio transmission that a convoy receiving sniper fire needed help. They were a klick from our location. We could hear automatic-weapons fire and faint explosions in the distance. We moved along the Red Ball, with second squad taking the lead. As we got closer, the sounds of weapons firing got louder.

We reached the convoy in no time and saw 10 vehicles stalled on the highway. The snipers were firing from a steep hill 250 feet high, with large boulders and thick vegetation, located west across the highway. Crouched behind a truck, Sergeant Stout and Lieutenant Baxter talked to the convoy commander, a young lieutenant. Then Sergeant Stout motioned for me to move up to their location.

I moved up and crouched next to Sergeant Stout, with the truck providing cover and concealment. The lieutenant said he saw three or four enemy soldiers. We continued to receive enemy fire.

Sergeant Stout said, "Haynie, fire your M-79 high-explosive rounds behind that group of boulders," as he pointed at the target 200 meters away.

I moved behind a jeep for cover and for a better view of the hillside. I pulled up my sight and adjusted for that distance. This being my first time firing the M-79, I felt that everyone was watching. They were! I loaded a grenade round, fired, and it fell short. I re-loaded, and the next round fell short, too. The third round was long. As I was firing, I could hear the zing of the AK-47 bullets as they passed overhead.

Sergeant Stout said, "Give me the weapon."

I replied, "No! I carry the damn thing, and I need to learn to fire it."

Sergeant Stout grinned and said, "Have at it, then." The fourth, fifth, and sixth rounds landed on target and exploded behind the boulders.

Sergeant Stout said, "Fire two more rounds."

I fired them on target. It got quiet.

As I was firing, Lieutenant Baxter asked for two volunteers to climb up the hill and check the NVA sniper position. Dennis Stout and Juan Ramos volunteered and moved up on the left flank toward the group of boulders. Lieutenant Baxter told everyone to hold their fire because two platoon members were working their way up to the sniper location.

Sergeant Stout asked, "Who volunteered?"

Lieutenant Baxter replied, "Ramos and your brother."

Sergeant Stout was pissed that his brother, Dennis, had volunteered; he'd told him earlier not to volunteer for dangerous assignments. Ramos and Dennis Stout crawled within range of the enemy position and threw several grenades into the same location I'd targeted. They moved to the position and found a blood trail but no enemy soldiers. They scrambled down the hill and re-joined the platoon.

The convoy commander thanked Lieutenant Baxter. Then his unit started up the vehicles and moved out along the highway. We stood around and watched the convoy until they were no longer visible. While waiting, I saw Sergeant Stout talking with Dennis. I couldn't hear what either one was saying, but it was obvious that the conversation turned heated by the way Sergeant Stout was waving his arms wildly as he talked. I'm sure it was not good for Dennis. We formed up and moved back into the vegetation to patrol along the Red Ball.

GOOD LUCK CHARM

As units passed each other, whether by convoy or walking, we raised our index and middle finger in the V sign—the peace sign meant "peace" and "going home"; it was a sign of solidarity with other GIs. So this symbol had meaning to us other than what it meant to the hippie culture. It was likely for a soldier to wear a peace-sign necklace or even a bracelet.

On the Red Ball, there were plenty of Coke girls around selling cold Cokes for 50 cents. They had bracelets and peace-sign necklaces for sale. They were young, wearing black or white "pajamas" and a straw hat for protection from the sun. I wanted a peace-sign necklace but didn't have cash with me. Paul Ponce noticed my dilemma, approached the Coke girl, and purchased the necklace for me. He made the purchase using broken English, broken Vietnamese, and sign language. He paid five dollars in Military Payment Certificates (MPC), which we thought of as Monopoly money. We didn't use United States currency in Vietnam.

Paul was always friendly, and his generosity didn't surprise me. There were many evenings we talked of "the world" and his wife while he did sit-ups and push-ups. He was getting in shape to meet his wife in Hawaii the next month on Rest and Recuperation (R & R).

I wore this necklace for the rest of my tour, and it became my lucky charm. Every time I got scared, I rubbed the necklace for luck. I rubbed off most of the design. I still have this necklace today, and every time I look at it, I have fond memories of Paul.

FREE-FIRE ZONE

We were still working the AO off the Red Ball and received a mission to remove residents from a village, including their livestock. Higher headquarters wanted to create a designated free-fire zone because this village was helping the VC and NVA and sympathized with their cause. Once the command had designated a specific geographical area as a free-fire zone, we could fire on any movement without checking or getting approval. The platoon received instructions not to give them time to pack but gather only what they could carry and move the villagers to another location. Because of what my training had taught me and from what I'd heard from platoon veterans about Vietnamese people, I'd become distrustful toward the Vietnamese population.

Entering the ville was like walking into a time machine and going back 100 years. There was no electricity, telephones, running water, or toilets. Huts made of grass and bamboo, circular in shape, with dirt floors, lined the trail. Others were raised two feet off the ground by short posts on each corner; they were rectangular in shape and had a wood floor. Several had c-ration cardboard on the sides for protection from the elements.

Children ran around half dressed, and the women wore black or white silk-like pajamas. Most wore a large conical hat made from straw that protected them from the sun. As we approached elderly women or men, they smiled at us, showing teeth that were stained black and red from chewing on "betel nut," a stimulant/drug that masqueraded as a nut. The villagers penned the livestock in, but we often saw pigs and chickens roaming free.

The smells were unexplainable: strange food, animals, rice paddies, and villagers merged into one scent, still foreign from what I was used to. There were only trails entering and leaving the ville and no nearby roads. More than 100 civilians lived here.

I moved from hut to hut, rounding up villagers, old women and men, and younger women with children. No teenage boys or young men were found. They'd enlisted in the South Vietnamese Army, the North Vietnamese Army, joined the VC, or went to the city for better-paying jobs. It became difficult to keep up with my platoon members and the villagers. The constant wailing, shouting, and movement distracted me. Organized chaos!

I moved to my last hut to remove the occupants and found an old woman, appearing to be about seventy years old, with grey hair, black teeth, and deep wrinkles on her face. She was wearing black pajamas and hiding in a corner, sitting on the floor. I yelled at her to get outside and move with the rest of the villagers. She didn't move until I approached her with my weapon pointing at her. I am sure I gave her a mean look, too. She started to walk, and at once I saw her walking with effort on two stumps right below her waist. Seeing her try to walk broke my heart. I understood what I was becoming. I picked her up; she spoke in Vietnamese and pointed to objects in her hut, but I ignored her appeal and carried her to her family.

After leaving her, I went back to the hut, got the objects (I do not remember the items), and brought them to her. Our eyes met, and I knew that she was afraid but thankful. I vowed not to be a cruel person, but how can you keep such a vow in war?

Once we had the villagers moving along the trail with their livestock to the new location, we received an order to burn the village. I took out my zippo lighter, flipped open the case, struck the wheel to start the flame, and held the flame next to the straw hut. The hut caught fire and burned. We used burning parts of one hut to ignite another hut. As the village burned, we moved out behind the villagers, herding them along the trail. After a while I looked back; large clouds of black smoke and flames were rising on the horizon. I took no pleasure in burning the village. The villagers looked back, too, and most wailed and cried, as they'd lost everything. We made sure they got to their new location and prevented anyone from returning. How sad because they'd lived here for hundreds of years. But . . . they deserved it, because they kept trying to kill us.

During the same week we moved through the rice paddies toward another village suspected of assisting and harboring the VC and NVA, an area known for its unfriendly (to US troops) civilian populace. We were on guard for anything out of the ordinary or villagers acting suspiciously. As we moved into the village, we noticed that there were 40 to 50 villagers huddled into the center of the village and acting scared. There were only old women and women with young children. Two Army of the Republic of Viet Nam (ARVN) soldiers stood guard over the group of villagers. Four Republic of Korea Armed Forces (ROK) soldiers stood to one side, talking and pointing to several people in the group of villagers.

This was the first time we'd seen ROK soldiers. We'd heard they were in the AO. They had reputations for being cruel. Several American advisors were with the ROK soldiers. Two ROK soldiers pulled several women out of the group and asked questions through an interpreter. Their voices became loud, and their body language—arms swinging with wild hand motions—suggested they were angry.

One ROK soldier grabbed a pregnant woman clutching a small male child, four years old and wearing only pants. He moved the woman to one side while another ROK soldier grabbed the child by the arm and moved him toward a well. An ROK soldier forced the pregnant woman to lie on the ground, and he pulled her shirt up to expose her swollen stomach. The second ROK soldier picked the child up and held him with his head facing into the well opening. He cried for his mother and tried to wiggle free from the ROK soldier's grasp. I thought the soldier would drop the child into the well if the child didn't stop fighting. The mother screamed for her child while the group of villagers cried and wailed.

An ROK soldier continued shouting at the pregnant woman, and the interpreter translated. The woman kept refusing to answer the questions but was screaming for her son's safety. The first ROK soldier then placed a heating tablet, used to heat rations, on her stomach and held a zippo lighter in the other hand, threatening to light the tablet while continuing to ask questions.

We passed through the village and acted as if nothing was wrong. I tried not to make eye contact with anyone: ARVNs, ROKs, or the American advisors. To this day I do not know if the ROK soldiers carried out their threats. I hope not. Does war make you lose your humanity?

RUN FROM A FIRE

In late May, we were still working off Highway 1. There was an enemy presence, including ambushes, sniper attacks, and NVA sightings. Our mission was to flush the enemy out. It was hotter than usual, and we hadn't received supplies in days. Our food and water supply was low. My last full meal had been twenty-four hours previous. I had one can of applesauce and a cup of water left in my canteen. We carried four to six quarts of water and three to five days of rations, so we needed resupply.

Captain Tyson called Lieutenant Baxter over the radio to change our mission. There was enemy movement reported on top of the mountain five klicks from our location. Helicopters would pick up the platoon and drop us off on the mountaintop. We cleared a landing zone by cutting and pushing the elephant grass against the ground and waited for the helicopters. Within an hour, three helicopters landed, and the First Platoon boarded the helicopters. We sat on the floor with our legs pulled in, our weapons between our legs, muzzles pointed downward. The policy was to have weapons on safe and the chamber empty of ammunition.

As the helicopters flew toward the mountaintop, I thought for sure this was a hot landing zone (enemy waiting). I'm sure everyone else did, too. Whenever we thought there was a hot landing zone, as I did that day, we ignored the rule and made sure our weapons had a bullet in the chamber. We reached our destination, and, as the helicopter circled the landing zone, we saw large plumes of smoke and fire started by the artillery and Huey gunship helicopters that had prepped the hilltop before we landed. I'm sure Lieutenant Baxter called in that there was a fire at the landing zone, but Lieutenant Colonel Ellis said the mission was a go.

The helicopters made a rapid descent to the landing zone, and those who hadn't already loaded a bullet in the chamber locked and loaded their weapons. We jumped off before the skids touched the ground, hitting the ground hard, fanning out to secure the landing zone. As the platoon gathered, the fire in the distance burned everything in its path behind and to both sides of our location. The flames climbed the trees and tall brush, and we heard the loud crackling of the burning wood. The thick, toxic smoke choked us.

We moved out toward the lone site without flames. As we moved through the jungle growth looking for the VC, we noticed the flames getting closer. The wind shifted, and there was plenty of fuel for the fire at our current location. The roar of the approaching flames grew louder as the flames seemed to reach to the sky. Flames singed our clothing, rucksacks, and hair as we ran, and the heat became unbearable. The squads were no longer in formation; we followed the person in front of us. Mike Dankert and I found ourselves together.

We ran along a trail and moved out of the fire's path. The platoon halted. Mike retrieved a can of pears from his rucksack, opened the can, and immediately sucked on the juice. He passed the can so I could share his drink—my first liquid in hours. After we'd drunk the pear juice, Mike shared the pears with me. Mike and I were afraid, and our fear seemed to produce some kind of silent communication and understanding between us. Without talking directly about what we would do if the fire caught us, we, nevertheless managed to agree to a plan of action. Without words, we knew what the other meant. Mike and I would not be burnt to death. We at once completely trusted each other. Mike and I began our friendship on this day.

Within minutes, the fire approached our location, finding more fuel to feed its flames, and we ran downwards along the mountainside. The wind kept changing direction. Lieutenant Baxter took the point position and led the platoon off the mountaintop, fighting thorn bushes and clearing the trail as he went. Several platoon members dropped their gear and screamed to move faster as the flames licked at our clothing and gear. We heard the panic in their voices. My throat was dry, and the fear kept my screams from escaping. As I ran, I forgot about the NVA—the fire was our enemy now. We made it to the bottom with no casualties. We found a stagnant pond at the bottom of the trail. I'm sure there was water-buffalo shit floating in that water. We dropped our equipment and weapons and knelt or lay on our stomachs to drink our first water in many hours and to wash the smoke from our eyes. No one got sick!

After a short period, we got the word to climb up the hill next to the one we had just left. From our position, it looked too high and steep. We were tired, hot, hungry, and thirsty, and we didn't want to make the climb. But we did. The platoon started the climb up and reached the top an hour before nightfall. Exhausted, we didn't give a shit if we ran into the enemy or not! If we had, it would've be a one-way battle, with us losing. I didn't have the strength to fight. Once we set up our positions, the supply chopper came in with food and water, just before the sun set behind the horizon. Something good was ending this disastrous day!

This is the letter Chuck Council wrote home to his parents in May of 1969. His Dad sent the letter to their U.S. Congressional Representative, Edith Green. She read the letter aloud on the floor of the U.S. Congress and entered it into the Congressional Record under the heading of "Troop Morale."

Dear Folks,

Today is Tuesday, I am sure of that but I am not sure if the date. I want to recount for you as best I can the events of last Saturday, May 24th.

Our company was shuttled by choppers to a nearby mountain ridge. (This is called a combat assault, CA). Running up and down the coast of Vietnam Nam is the country's only major road. Known as Highway Number One or the "Red Ball." We use the Red Ball extensively for moving truck convoys and during the past couple of weeks numerous of convoys have been getting ambushed along the highway. Our company was lifted to the west of the Red Ball and was to sweep east attempting to flush out snipers. On the east side of the ridge and the west side were brush fires and they dropped us right in between them. Due to our position we had to move north down across a small valley and then uphill again to another ridge top. And the fire was burning right in our heels. Everyone was covered with soot and cinders and the sun shone yellow through the smoke. The heat was intense and the fire made it noticeably hotter. We reached the second ridge top and everyone hoped that we would get some sanctuary from the fire. We already had taken a couple of heat casualties but nothing serious so far.

We had no more than dropped our gear then strong gusty winds whipped the fire up towards our position. The word went out to move down to the Red Ball which was directly below us but we were so high up that it looked ten miles down. This time we moved due east down the side of the mountain through semi-jungle vegetation. Do you have any idea how thick "semi-jungle "vegetation is? It didn't matter much at the time because the fire had closed in so rapidly the company was in near panic. I was up towards the front and we could hear those in the back yelling to move faster. But we were in high gear as it was. If the fire had gotten onto the east slope of that mountain, well, Alpha Company would be no more. It took two hours to move our way down to the Red Ball through the heavy foliage. When the whole company was finally down all kinds of gear and ammo were missing. We had something around a dozen heat casualties and the worst part was we didn't have any water as it had been almost 24 hours since our last resupply. Somebody found a nearby stagnant pond and everybody began drinking water, stagnant water. As far as I know no one has gotten sick from that water, but we were just lucky, that's all. By this time it was about mid-afternoon. There is no effective way to describe the total and complete exhaustion that we all experienced. Not only from the physical exhaustion but the intense fear of being caught in that fire.

Now comes the killer, we received orders from battalion to move back up and secure that same ridge top overlooking the Red Ball. The company at that point reflected the epitome of demoralization. We moved out later in the afternoon and step by agonizing step worked our way back up the same slopes that had earlier chased us off by fire. I want to tell you, that night when we finally reached the top of that hill I was just about at the end of the line. Not from just fatigue but morale-wise too. I didn't give a dam about anything and most others felt the same as me.

Three days later we are still sitting on the same mountain top with the purpose of observing truck convoys passing below us. They brought up an 81mm mortar with the hope of zeroing in quickly on any snipers that may start shooting at convoys. Our company is providing security for the mountain. But Charlie is no idiot unlike most of our military people. He knows exactly what we are up here for so yesterday the VC moved their ambush site to the north out of our range and attacked 3 convoys. But we go on about our work of securing this hill, clearing brush, laying barbed wire and digging gun positions. Probably within a week or so we'll move off the hill and all of our work will have been for nothing. "Mine is not to question why, mine is to do or die."

In your last letter you made some statement about dropping an atomic bomb on North Vietnam. It has become my opinion that our best course of action would be just the opposite. Pack up and get the hell out of this God forsaken place. I do not know one GI over here who would trade even as much as a single teaspoon of US soil for this entire country. I sincerely feel that just the mere presence of U.S. Military Forces is doing more to perpetuate this war than any other single factor. I am not a conscientious objector because I cannot say that all wars are futile, but this one is futile. If I should die over here there is no way that you could justify or anyone could justify the loss of my life, I have not seen or even heard of any military objective over here that warrants the loss of a single American life. The propaganda argument that we are fighting for our country in Vietnam is the biggest bunch of shit I have ever heard. If you were over here and could see the way the people respond to us and the way we respond to them you would fully understand. I also fail to see how aggressive Communism in a backwards very primitive country like Vietnam on the other side of the world poses a threat to the security to the United States.

I guess I have raked Vietnam over the coals long enough. The manner in which the army conducts operations in Vietnam and just the fact that we are in Vietnam in the first place it is quite easy for me to understand why there is so much dissent and rebellion among the youth of our country today. The resentment is deep and it is going to get worse before it gets better. Frankly, I am resentful against my commanding officers for some of their decisions and orders. I place too much value on my life to allow the U.S. Army to sacrifice it for some obscure and totally meaningless objective in Vietnam. I think this is perhaps at least part of the root of the rebellion against the "military industrial complex" of today. Gotta go for now. Write later.

Love, Chuck

PS. Please send me one dozen packages of unsweetened Kool-Aid. All flavors except lime.

This is an excerpt from a letter Lieutenant John Baxter wrote to his parents May 25, 1969, about the mission that day.

Well our mission changed yesterday. And to sum it up yesterday was just one hell of a day. We hiked 3.5 km in mountains yesterday morning before we got a call to change missions. Then we sat in a hot mountain meadow awaiting choppers. We had a combat assault near the red ball Hy#1. 10 minutes later fires started in the dry brush and woods from artillery which prepped the area just before we landed. The fires literally chased us out of the hills to the red ball. It was the scaredest I've been yet because I was afraid the fires would catch us. There was no trail off the hill about 170m high & we literally dove off the hill. I took over as lead man part of the way crashing through 10 ft. high thorn bushes. All this time we had no water & it was 100+ in the sun and the heat of the fire. We made it to the bottom safely only a couple of heat casualties but they were all right after a few hours. Then after finding water we had to push back up another 140 m hill to spend the night. We covered some 10km all day 3km at breakneck speed. All this with packs over 65 lbs. So needless to say we were an exhausted bunch. But when we got to the top of the last hill a chopper came with water and mail 3 letters plus Kool-Aid and cigars. Just as well we are holding our position today as I have a stiff knee . . . Well so much for another day in Vietnam. I just hope we don't have to go thru another like it.

The company alerted the platoon that the supply chopper was coming in, so we stayed vigilant, watching to our front to make sure we engaged anyone who fired on the Huey while it landed. Sergeant Stout popped smoke and verified the color of smoke to the pilot to show the chopper our location and then guided it in to land at the best spot. Thank God we are getting food and water. We could never mistake the helicopter blades cutting through the air "whoop, whoop, whoop" at a distance out. Even today a helicopter flying gets my attention.

First the supply chopper hovered over the landing zone so the rubber bladder containing water could be unhooked. Once the crew released the water container, the Huey landed, the crew members kicked out the platoon's supplies and departed. We picked up the supplies and moved them back to the CP location. We took turns going to the water container to fill our canteens. I was now carrying six quarts of water every day, two one-quart and two of the two-quart canteens.

The platoon received cases of C-Rations, Sundries Packs (SP Packs), ammunition, and water to last for three days. We used the barrels of our M-16s to break the wire around the C-Ration cases, and Sergeant Stout turned the case upside down so no one in the squad could identify the meal by the label. Squad members took turns selecting the number of meals required. The meals came in by the case, sealed by wire, containing twelve meals. There were three types of meals, B1, B2 or B3, and each case had four of each. The Army stored food items in labeled brown cans and placed them in a light brown box that had the food group and meal name on the box lid. A box contained a meat, fruit, crackers with peanut butter and jelly or cheese, and cake or candy bar. An accessory pack in each meal contained instant coffee, creamer, gum, cigarettes, matches, toilet paper, plastic spoon, salt, pepper and sugar. We traded and went through the discarded C-rations to find our favorites.

I always ate the B3 meals, which had the Beef Spiced with Sauce and Chicken Noodle meal; both these meals came with a package of Cocoa Beverage Powder for hot chocolate. I didn't drink coffee. These meals were my favorites. In each case were four P-38 can openers. Supposedly, the name "P-38" originated in the fact that it took 38 punctures or turns of the handle to open a can.

An SP Pack was a box that contained writing material, with envelopes, and toiletries, including shaving cream, razor, soap, toothbrush, and toothpaste. The pack contained cigarettes and other tobacco products (pipe tobacco and cigars), matches, lighter fluid, and "John Wayne" candy bars. They got the name because we figured the only person who could eat them was John Wayne. There were hard candies, Life Savers, and Charms and gum chuckles. The SP Pack was for 100 soldiers, and we received a pack for the platoon, which was only 25 soldiers. What we didn't use, we buried or burned with the discarded C-rations.

We distributed the ammunition based on what each person needed. There was enough for everyone. We received a ration of two Cokes and two beers each time a supply chopper came out. I always traded my beer for Coke. I'd learned my lesson about drinking beer!

Getting clean clothes, though rarely, the supply helicopter dropped them off in a huge bundle. The bundle contained uniforms, underclothes, and socks. The veterans picked a complete uniform first, and the newbies picked a uniform from the leftovers. This concerned me because I'd lost so much weight that the smallest size was still too big for me. The small-size shirt and pants were in high demand. Most soldiers didn't wear underclothes. I received the small-size shirt and pants; the veterans felt sorry for me and let me have them.

The best item in the resupply chopper was mail. We did not receive mail every day, but everyone looked forward to getting a letter. We looked forward to anyone who received a package from home. I can't think of anyone who didn't share his goodies from home. We placed our outgoing mail in a pouch going to the rear to be mailed. The helicopter came back to pick up the rubber bladder, dirty uniforms, and the ammunition we didn't need.

I compiled a list to show what the average rifleman carried every day.

Rucksack

Pistol Belt with Ammo Pouch and two first aid bandages

Poncho

Poncho Liner

Steel pot (helmet with liner)

M-16 Rifle

14 Loaded Magazines of 5.56 Ammunition, worn tied around the body in the cloth bandoleers the ammo comes in

10 Boxes (to reload in 10 empty magazines) 5.56 Ammunition in Rucksack

2 Hand Grenades

1 Concussion Grenade

1 Smoke Grenade

1 Claymore Mine

100 rounds of M-60 Ammunition

1 M72 Light Anti-Tank Weapon (LAW)

2 Trip Flares

1 lb. of C-4—Matches and Lighter

6 Quarts water (two 2-quart canteens and two 1-quart canteens)

9 cans of beef with spice sauce/chicken noodle—P-38 can opener and Plastic Spoon

9 cans of fruit

9 cans of cake

6 cans of peanut butter, jelly and crackers

6 packets of cocoa

2 LRRP, pronounced "LURP," Meals when we could get them

2 cans of soda/beer—Can/Bottle Opener

Water Purification tablets

Malaria pills

Insect Repellent

1 Extra Pair of Socks

Toothbrush, soap, toilet paper

Any personal items a soldier wanted to carry

PAY DAY

Even in the field, on a firebase, wounded at a hospital, or at stand-down, we received our monthly pay. We received our pay on the last day of the month or on the last Friday of the month, whichever came first. We received pay once a month. I was a Private First Class, a pay grade of E-3, and my salary with combat pay was $200 a month. We didn't pay federal income tax while in Vietnam. We didn't have a check to bank but could set up an allotment to have our money sent to a person or institution. I had $150 sent to my bank savings account for deposit each month. After my tour, the money I'd saved and won from poker games allowed me to buy my first car, a 1968 Cutlass Supreme Oldsmobile with a V8 350 engine.

On payday an officer flew to our location with two armed guards carrying a company roster, a locked leather satchel, and Olive Drab (OD) green wooden field table and chair. The pay officer this month was Lieutenant Baxter. First, he unfolded and set up the table and chair; then he unlocked and opened the satchel full of MPC currency. We lined up in front of his table by squad. My turn came, and I approached the pay officer and reported by saluting and stating, "Sir, Private Haynie reports for pay." There was no requirement for the pay officer to return the salute. This was the only time we saluted an officer in the field. Lieutenant Baxter checked my name against the list and then he counted out my pay. He deducted the monthly dues for the beer and Coke fund. I picked up my money, saluted, and moved back to my position. I placed my cash in my plastic American Division wallet, issued to me at the Combat Center. The only time we spent our MPC was on stand-down, playing poker or purchasing from a Coke Girl. Once the pay officer paid the company, he locked the satchel, closed up his table and chair, boarded back on the helicopter, and flew to the next company location. The platoon leaders liked getting this duty because it got them out of the field for a week.

This is an excerpt from a letter Lieutenant John Baxter wrote to his parents May 30, 1969, and June 2, 1969, about being the pay officer.

I'm in LZ Bronco as pay officer. So this means a week out of the field and running around paying people-in the field on firebases and the hospital in Chu Lai . . . Also my legs are all bandaged up one from "jungle rot" open sores but they are healing well the other for strained ligaments & fluid on the knee . . . few more days taking it easy should settle that . . . a good project for those in G'ville who'd like to "help the boys in 'Nam'." There is a lack of reading material in the company paperbacks, Westerns, mysteries and "pop" novels are all read and enjoyed.

"..still paying people 6 chopper rides yesterday, 2 today and a flight to Chu Lai tomorrow to get the hospitals . . . experienced my first big rocket attack last night. It is a horrifying sound that I'll probably never forget. Break-I've just spent the last 2 hours in a bunker we had a mortar attack no damage. Maybe I should go back to the field where it is safer."

Figure 4 First Sergeant Malpica at Fire Support Base Bronco. Photo provided by Chuck Council.

Figure 5 Alpha Company Officers. CPT Tyson, LT Baxter, LTC Ellis, LT Ehrich, LT Wood for Lieutenant Baxter Promotion to 1LT. Photo provided by John Baxter.

Figure 6 FSB Charlie Brown view of China Sea and Village. Photo provided by Tom Powell.

Figure 7 Bridge on Highway 1(Red Ball). Note positions on each side of bridge manned by first and second squad of First Platoon. Photo provided by Leslie Pressley.

Figure 8 Mike Dankert on the Beach. Note the two graves behind and to the left of him. Photo provided by Mike Dankert.

Figure 9 Dennis Stout guard duty on LZ Cork. Photo provided by Dennis Stout.

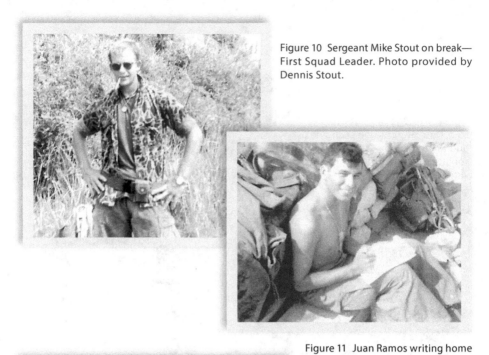

Figure 10 Sergeant Mike Stout on break—First Squad Leader. Photo provided by Dennis Stout.

Figure 11 Juan Ramos writing home from the Bridge. Photo provided by Dusty Rhoades.

Figure 12 Maurice Harrington, Joe Mitchell, Sergeant Mike Stout on LZ Debbie. Photo provided by Dennis Stout.

Figure 13 Paul Ponce and Leslie Pressley at FSB Bronco (Duc Pho). Photo provided by Leslie Pressley.

Figure 14 Peace sign given by Paul Ponce to Glyn Haynie. It became Glyn's good-luck charm.

Figure 15 Resupply Chopper(Huey) being unloaded. Photo provided by John Baxter.

Figure 16 Resupply Chinook helicopter with fresh water. Photo provided by John Baxter.

CHAPTER 4

NO LONGER THE NEW GUY

The end of May and first week of June, the platoon received ten new replacements and two more at the end of June. This brought the unit's strength higher than it had been in a long time. Most were 20-year-old draftees. June was the first of several tough months; the platoon saw a soldier killed in action (KIA) and several wounded in action (WIA). Getting new replacements was always hard because that meant we lost experienced people to rear jobs, casualties, or normal rotation from the field. The new replacements who came in at the end of May and early June were John DeLoach, Ray Hamilton, Sergeant Ronald Owens, Sergeant Jerry Zwiesler, Ryan Okino, Barry Suda, Charlie Deppen, Robert Smith, Bill Davenport (see Appendix D), and our new platoon sergeant Staff Sergeant Robert Swindle. Danny Carey and Frank Brown arrived near the end of June.

THE POINT MAN

Juan Ramos carried the M-79 grenade launcher as his assigned weapon, and this wasn't a desirable weapon to carry for most. It fired only one 40mm grenade at a time, which needed to travel 30 meters before the round armed and was able to explode, or you could fire a canister round. But it was an important weapon for the squad. Being the new guy, Juan gave me the M-79, and he took my M-16. I reluctantly carried the M-79 for a month until Lieutenant Baxter assigned a replacement to the squad by the name of John DeLoach. John was from Mississippi, so that became his nickname. He was tall at six feet, two inches, with an easygoing disposition. John was several months younger than me, so I was no longer the youngest member of the platoon. I asked John if he would carry the M-79, and I would carry his M-16. He agreed.

I convinced Lieutenant Baxter to assign the M-79 to Mississippi, and I volunteered to walk point for the platoon. This was how I got the job as point man for the first platoon, and I walked point for the rest of my tour. With training, I became good at the task and preferred to be up front.

The soldier walking point was entrusted with the safety of the sol- diers behind him. He led the platoon through the jungle, along trails, across streams, and through open fields during daytime, nighttime, and inclement weather. He needed to know the direction—not a location— to lead the unit. The point man looked for signs of the enemy, such as ambushes and booby traps, so he could alert the platoon to impending danger. It didn't always work out that way. He was usually the first person to make contact with a sniper or enemy soldier. Sometimes the enemy let the point man walk through an ambush so the main body of the unit got hit. The point man needed to develop awareness for impending danger.

HAD TO HITCHHIKE TO GET THERE

After being in-country for three months, I took a seven-day leave and was happy that the First Sergeant could schedule my absence. Every soldier was allowed a seven-day R & R (did not count against leave time) and a seven-day leave during his tour of duty. Going on leave, we flew standby and got to go to whatever destination was available. Several destinations were: Australia, Tokyo, Bangkok, Manila, and Hong Kong, to name a few. I wanted to go to Australia.

The platoon was working off Highway 1 and firebase Debbie. On the day I needed to leave, I reminded Lieutenant Baxter that I needed to get on the first supply chopper back to FSB Bronco, the Brigade FSB.

Lieutenant Baxter said, "Captain Tyson said there will not be any supply choppers for several days. If you want to go, you can walk back to FSB Bronco."

I said, "Hell, yes! I will do that, Sir."

A soldier from another platoon and I walked east several klicks across the rice paddies and through hedgerows to Highway 1. Once we reached the highway, we headed north and kept walking until a convoy came. As a convoy approached, we waved to get their attention. It worked—they stopped.

The soldier with me asked, "Can you give us a ride to FSB Bronco?"

"Sure. Get in the back of the truck," replied a sergeant.

We both said, "Thanks" at the same time.

We ran around to the back of the truck and threw our gear over the tailgate. Then we climbed on and found a seat. The back of the truck held ammunition. As soon as we took a seat, the truck moved forward and headed north toward Bronco.

Once we'd arrived at Bronco and the truck stopped, I grabbed my gear and climbed out of the back of the truck. I walked to the company headquarters, checked in with the First Sergeant, showered, and changed into a clean uniform. I packed a small bag. Rules required we travel in Khaki uniform while leaving and returning to the field and wear civilian clothes at the R & R destination. I got a flight out of FSB Bronco on a C-130 to Da Nang. I checked in and found no seats available for two days. The heck with that! I caught another flight on a C-130 to Saigon. I again checked in and found the only available flight was to Tokyo the next morning. So I agreed to that flight; it wasn't Australia—but it wasn't Vietnam, either.

The time was 1900 hours, so I ventured to downtown Saigon for the evening. The city was bustling with nightlife; the streets were lighted, and there were many bars. I heard the sounds of American music and laughter. I ventured into a bar for a drink. Once I was seated, a woman came to my table, sat in a chair, told me how handsome I was, and asked me to buy her a drink. She was my age, wearing a mini-skirt, a revealing blouse, and heavy applied makeup. The idea was to get you drunk and to keep buying her drinks at one to two dollars a drink served in a shot glass. The drink was nothing more than a Kool-Aid flavored drink, called "Saigon Tea" by the patrons of the bars. She downed the drink, wanting another. Selling Saigon Tea was profitable for them. Once you were out of money, they moved on to the next table. I was on my way to Tokyo, so I waited on any invitations for conversations (or any other offer). I went back to base and spent the night, sleeping in a chair at the departure section to be ready to catch my flight the next morning. I caught my flight; I was headed for seven days in Tokyo.

On the flight over, I talked with the soldier sitting next to me. We were the same age, and he was a grunt from the 1st Infantry Division. David was six feet tall and 165 pounds. He had been in Vietnam longer than me. We landed, got through customs and the briefing, and went to the same hotel. The cab ride was a harrowing experience, but we made it.

We got checked in, changed to civilian clothes and headed to the bar. After two drinks, David said he felt ill and had a fever. Later in the evening, he felt worse. He had uncontrollable shivering, a spike in his fever, and he was sweating profusely. I got a cab and took him to the closest military hospital. The doctors diagnosed David with malaria, and he remained in the hospital until he got better. I felt sorry for him, but now I was on my own.

Once back at the hotel, I packed up his belongings, checked him out of the hotel, and took his luggage to the hospital the next day. I spent my seven days visiting David at the hospital during the day and heading to the bars at night. The bars in Tokyo were similar to Vietnam. A girl dressed in mini-skirt and revealing blouse sat at my table telling me how much she admired me and how handsome I was as she asked for more drinks. She was so convincing I believed her! As it got near closing time, she disappeared. I headed back to my hotel alone. My visit to Tokyo was OK but not too exciting. At least I'd gotten away from the field and had had hot meals, showers, and clean clothes. My trip back to the platoon was uneventful, and I was glad to see the platoon members again. I never saw David again.

This is an excerpt from a letter Charlie Deppen wrote to his mother and father, dated June 11 and 12, 1969.

Right now I am sitting on a hill overlooking the Redball (Highway 1). Last night we saw about fifteen enemy in the open and called in artillery fire. I don't know yet if we got any of them. The worst thing about this action is the waiting and the boredom, and the insects and heat don't add much.... By the way, I thought of something you could send me in your letters. Since the water here usually tastes pretty bad, some pre-sweetened Kool-Aid would help. If you would put about two packs in each letter, I would appreciate it.

... I had to go on patrol so I could not finish the letter yesterday.... Dad, your letter of June 3 gave me food for thought. It's good to know that loved one's are thinking of you and this case is no exception. I will try to hang in there like you did. Right now I'm trying to make a big decision which would mean a change of MOS for me. Whatever I decide I will have given it due thought. So just hope to make the right decision....

BE GENTLE—JUNE 13–14

We were still working around highway 1, which continued to have a VC and NVA presence. We were moving in the low areas, checking villages for weapons and food caches. In the late afternoon, we moved to the high ground overlooking the valley below, and we stopped on the top of the highest point to set up our perimeter for the night. The hilltop was flat and large, too big for one platoon to cover effectively. The CP group manned a position on the perimeter; normally they were in the center of the perimeter. Lieutenant Baxter assigned the positions for the best use of the terrain. My position had a 40-foot clearing to the front, with rocks jutting up two inches high, scattered across the clearing that ran downhill into the dense overgrowth, which was so thick that there was no way we could see anyone approaching.

Sergeant Stout told Ponce and me to set up claymores and trip flares to our front. Ponce and I moved to the front of our position into the overgrowth. We set up four claymore mines and three trip flares where we determined likely avenues of approach by the enemy to our position. Ponce and I ran the wire for the claymores back to our position and connected the clickers to the wire. We were ready.

I settled in with my best meal of the day: beef with spice sauce, peanut butter and jelly with crackers crunched together, a can of pears, pound cake, and Kool-Aid. After eating, I heated a cup of hot chocolate and then walked over to Mike's position to visit. We talked how I had hitched-hiked out of the field and my Tokyo trip. There were many times, since the fire, during breaks or before nightfall, that Mike and I would talk about "the world" and our families or our squads and what we had been doing. As we talked, the sun faded, and the dreaded nighttime approached. How I hated the night. I told Mike I would see him later and moved back to my position.

Sergeant Stout set up the guard rotation: Himself, Ramos, Ponce, and me—I wasn't on until next to last, after Ponce. I wrapped up in my poncho liner, fluffed my rucksack for a pillow, and went to sleep.

From a deep sleep, I found myself low crawling toward the center of the perimeter. There was a loud explosion with a flash of light and small-arms fire. Damn! I was crawling without my rifle. I crawled back, retrieved my rifle, and with the rest of the squad, returned fire into the blackness. We received more small-arms fire at our position. I got into a sitting position to see the front better and to give accurate fire at the enemy. Sergeant Stout looked to his left and saw me exposed and firing at the flashes of light in the dense overgrowth.

He yelled, "Haynie—get down!"

I hit the ground, lying as flat as possible. As bullets zinged over our heads like a swarm of angry bees, I looked at Sergeant Stout and said, "Thanks." I thought, *What the hell? Exposing myself—what a stupid FNG mistake!* A second explosion erupted at the same position to my right. I knew then it was Mike's position that got hit the hardest.

Sergeant Stout shouted, "Throw your grenades to the front!" Everyone at our position lobbed grenades downhill, and the light from the exploding grenades blinded us. As our vision cleared, we continued to fire into the darkness. We squeezed the triggers to discharge the four claymore mines placed at suspected entry points to our position. This took the pressure off us. We continued to fire at any movement we thought was the enemy for another 15 minutes.

Spooky, a converted C-47 with mini-guns and flares, arrived while we were waiting for the dust-off. Spooky dropped flares to light the perimeter and help us locate any VC still in the vicinity; it sprayed mini-gun fire around our perimeter. The light was not perfect but enough to distinguish between the shadows and the enemy. Spooky stayed the night with us, circling and dropping flares. I was so thankful for the pilot for staying with us and giving enough light for us to see.

A dust-off landed, and second-squad members loaded the two most seriously wounded, VanDyke and Rowe, both from second squad. The dust-off departed and flew to the Division Hospital at Chu Lai.

A second dust-off helicopter landed, and I observed four figures throw a person onto the helicopter floor. I thought, *My God—be gentle placing that wounded soldier on the helicopter!* They moved as fast as possible so the helicopter could head to the hospital. Then I saw a platoon member climb into the dust-off. The second dust-off took off and flew to the Brigade Hospital at Duc Pho.

We stayed awake the night, waiting and watching for the enemy. We prepared to engage the enemy with any shadow we saw or sound we heard. I lay on my stomach with my M-16 pointed to the front of our position, not even thinking of sleep—only the enemy. Sweat rolled down my face, and my mouth was dry. I needed water, but I dared not move. Every several minutes I would shiver; I didn't know if it was the cool breeze against my sweating body or fear. It was a long night.

After daybreak I talked with second squad members and found out that the soldier was dead, not wounded. It was Bruce Tufts, the soldier I'd first met and earlier described as resembling a Viking. I asked Pressley about Mike, and he told me his wound wasn't as serious as the other two; he had taken shrapnel in the upper arm, and he had left on the chopper with Tufts. Mike came back to the platoon two days later. Dennis Rowe and Nick VanDyke never returned to the platoon; they went back to the States.

We had breakfast like any other morning, but it was quiet, no joking or horsing around like usual. Lieutenant Baxter gave the order to move out, with first squad in the lead. We discovered several enemy dead and blood trails as we were moving off the hilltop. The claymores had done their job. We found a dead NVA soldier riddled with claymore pellets. The squad stopped, and we stared at the NVA soldier. One squad member lowered an M-16, pointed it at a dead NVA soldier's head, and emptied a twenty-round magazine into his face. We watched as his face and head disappeared. We stared at the body. The squad was quiet and somber. I didn't give a shit—he most likely had killed Tufts. Then we continued moving along the trail, acting as if nothing had happened.

This was my first experience losing a platoon member or having a platoon member wounded. The realization struck me that any of us could be killed or wounded any time. I hated the NVA and VC!

This is an excerpt from a letter Lieutenant Baxter wrote to a friend, dated June 17, 1969.

"2 years from the day I returned to the US from Chile-Seems like a long time ago. It has been a long and unhappy week. I've been back in the field 8 days and we've seen our share of action. Today we got hot chow & cold beer out here for the first time . . . While all this might seem trite to those in the world they mean a lot to us here."

This is an excerpt from a letter Lieutenant Baxter wrote to his parents, dated June 17, 1969.

"Well another week has gone by—we're out guarding Hwy #1 again in a different location. It has been rather rough especially as it seem to be getting hotter . . .Water resupply is a continual logistical problem but somehow we make it . . . due to go a firebase for a while"

This is a letter from Charlie Deppen to his mother and father, dated June 20, 1969.

Dear Mom and Dad,

We are no longer with the Company element. The past few days have been absurd since we sit up in the hills during the day and wait until after dark to start down. The trails are rocky, steep, and very treacherous. We have already had one sprained ankle, and I'm lucky I don't have one too.

Today we went into a village to wash up, shave, and get water (tastes bad, but it's all we have). We also bought three cases of cokes from the local entrepreneurs ($10-$12 per case with ice). The ville is scenic but dirty. The most depressing thing is to see huts made of bamboo poles with tin siding or siding of old C-ration boxes. The children are friendly and crowd around you asking for chop-chop (food). Although there are many young children, you never see men of military age (they are either in a big town, VC or ARVN (loyalist troops).

I already have a small dose of jungle rot on my hands. Any scratch gets infected since you can't keep clean out in the bush.

The areas are small (just scratches) so it's only bothersome and not too bad. This is just part of being a soldier in Vietnam.

Glad to hear the Lake Charles job is finally under way. I hope you get the other job in that area.

We pulled guard every night. I think about playing bridge to keep awake. I also categorize the different things I'm going to drink when I get home. Milk heads the list, then there are juices (orange, grape, grapefruit, pineapple, apple and lemonade), soft drinks (about six types), mixed drinks, Kool-Aid, water, and root beer floats. Not very interesting, but the saliva keeps me awake. If I slept, I'd drown in it. Write me soon and say hi to Lucille and Harriet.

Love, Charles

FIRST STAND-DOWN

At the end of June, Battalion scheduled our company for stand-down. Every Infantry combat unit in our Division got to go on stand-down every 60 to 90 days. Our stand-down was in Chu Lai, the Division Firebase, allowing the company three days of rest and recuperation from the constant exposure to the elements and fear—this kind of rest was something we didn't get very often. We were in a fenced compound within the Division firebase, but we could come and go as we please. During the three days, we ate steak for all three meals; we drank, slept, played poker, and listened to bands. And drank some more. We got hot showers and clean clothes, and got to sleep on a mattress. We went to the Post Exchange (PX) to buy film, cameras, and watches. These items weren't available anywhere else. The Class VI store was where we purchased liquor. Normally there was live music from a Korean or Filipino band singing pop songs in broken English. We could be a rowdy bunch of soldiers. Our motto was: "What are you going to do, send us to Nam?"

The platoon loaded into a Chinook helicopter and departed to Chu Lai for stand-down. Once we landed, the rear door lowered, and we moved off toward a group of buildings and a large container used as an arms room. We lined up in front of the container and turned in our weapons, ammunition, and any other explosives we were carrying. Once we'd turned in our weapons, we moved to an assigned building that housed bunks and lockers. Each squad member selected a bunk and stored their gear. Three things became important to me: Safety, food, and sleep in that order.

The mess hall set up grills and grilled steaks from the morning hours through the night. They had every type of food available—and desserts. Stacked next to the mess hall were pallets of beer and soda, and next to the pallets were coolers full of ice, beer, and soda.

It was during these three days that Mike and I had more time to associate together, and we quickly became good friends. We played one-on-one basketball, drank Jim Beam, and sat around and talked about our home life, high school, and friends. We talked several times about the fire. Mike and I found we had a great deal in common. While eating our steak dinners, the conversation turned to our squads, the different people in each, and how our squad leaders took care of us. It's strange how squads mingled little in the field.

Each night Mike and I got together and listened to a band playing current songs and sipped on our drinks, bourbon, and Coke. The last song any band played was "We Gotta Get Out of This Place" by The Animals, a downer song to close the night. I played in the continuous poker game while Mike watched. He filled my glass with bourbon and Coke while I played. Mike made sure I made it back to my bunk after the game. I drank too much but won a lot of money.

Although I'd been with the platoon for only less than two months, it felt good to let your guard down and relax. The three days went by quickly. We picked up our weapons, ammunition, and explosives and loaded into the Chinook to head back to the field. The Chinook landed in the same vicinity, Highway 1, we were working before stand-down. Once the rear door dropped, we rapidly departed the helicopter and moved into the thick vegetation for cover and concealment. We are ready for another 60 to 90 days in the field—no longer safe, eating C-rations, and getting little sleep.

HIRED KILLERS

In late June we loaded onto the Huey helicopters and flew to Firebase Debbie for a company rotation—the first time on Debbie for me and Mike. To the platoon veterans, Debbie was a familiar setup; they'd occupied Debbie earlier. It was Alpha Company's turn to secure the FSB. It was on top of a steep, rocky mountain, as opposed to a hill. Looking east you could see the South China Sea and, west, the villages and rice-paddy fields. Lieutenant Baxter assigned three to four squad members to a bunker. From the assigned bunker, we pulled security for the firebase. Several nights we moved downhill along the steep slope several hundred meters from the bunker line to set up ambushes. We had showers, a mess hall, and a latrine—more than we had in the field.

These are excerpts from letters that Lieutenant Baxter wrote to his parents June 23, 1969, and June 26, 1969, and an excerpt from a letter to a friend June 26, 1969.

23 June letter to parents

My platoon has been operating on its own for the last couple of weeks. It has been pretty hairy at times but the kids have performed pretty well. I've sure got a lot of new green ones-some are activated National Guard . . .Nixon's plan of getting us out suits me. The NVA show no signs of quitting-the VC in this area has been pretty much neutralized. The NVA are taking high losses but they still attack the big bases. I figure they want us to leave with our tails between our legs . . .head to firebase tomorrow.

26 June letter to parents

. . . We're on a firebase now for a few days-LZ Debbie. We'll be here a few days pulling mostly daily missions. We can certainly use the rest.

26 June letter to a friend

... Nixon's plans about bringing troops home sure sounds
good. However NVA show no signs of easing up, they're trying to
hurt us badly so that it looks like we're surrendering ... Though
my overall feelings about this war are unchanged. You can't help
feel a little ruthless & hateful i.e. eye for eye when you see your
people messed up & hear of friends & OCS classmates being killed.
Excuse the writing-PEACE IN VIETNAM!

Once on the firebase, the Battalion tasked Alpha Company to sweep
the vicinity outside the Rice Bowl, so named because it had a bowl shape
containing rice paddies and surrounded by hills covered in jungle
growth. The aim was to move the enemy into an ARVN unit acting as
a blocking force. My first thought was, *Why couldn't we be the blocking
force and the ARVN units do the sweep?* It sounded fair to me. It appeared
the ARVN units always got the easier part of any mission.

The platoon moved to the firebase helicopter pad and waited for
the Hueys arriving for the pickup. As soon as they landed, the platoon
boarded the Hueys. The three helicopters lifted off, First Platoon out
first, and dropped us at the landing zone the company commander had
established as the starting point for the sweep. Once on the ground, we
provided security for the landing zone. The rest of the company soon
arrived, and we moved forward with First Platoon taking the lead.

The platoon moved methodically through the thick brush and
elephant grass. Once we spotted the enemy, we opened fire. We
continued to move forward, drawing fire and returning fire, still
pushing the enemy back. I had only the elephant grass and brush
for concealment but no cover for the incoming rounds. After several
hours of this cat-and-mouse approach, the enemy moved into the
ARVN blocking force positions, which opened fire on the enemy. The
company now had them in a crossfire, and the firefight continued for
30 minutes. Then it got quiet. The enemy disappeared through the

ARVN line without being detected. There were seven NVA dead, and weapons recovered.

First Platoon secured the landing zone and was the last platoon to leave. The Hueys landed and picked up the company with no enemy interference. After the platoons were back on Debbie, Lieutenant Colonel Ellis had everyone in the company gather around, and he announced "There's a steak dinner waiting for my hired killers."

Mike and I moved through the chow line, loaded our trays with food, and each selected a steak. We sat together for the hot meal, and I said, "I'm not sure the announcement pleased me, but I appreciate the steak."

The next day Captain Tyson assigned the platoon to work with a Vietnamese Provincial Force unit. We loaded onto the helicopters and flew from Debbie to a village in the Rice Bowl. We landed outside the village and met up with a combat engineer team, APCs, and the Provincial Force. The platoon mission was to give security while the Provincial Force troops searched the village for VC, weapons, and tunnels. It was high time that *they* did the work and *we* watched!

We observed the Vietnamese force soldiers moving from hut to hut, searching for VC or weapons. They searched the surrounding vicinity for tunnels and bunkers. They searched as we sat with the APCs, ensuring their safety. To their credit they captured five VC and found a weapons cache with ammunition. Engineers destroyed tunnels and bunkers, and First Platoon didn't help in the search.

Our mission turned out to be an easy one for us. Once the engineers blew the tunnels, we loaded on the helicopters and headed back to Debbie. I wished more of our missions were this easy, letting the Vietnamese forces do most of the dirty work, and we watch. It appeared it was always the other way around working with Vietnamese units.

This is a letter from Charlie Deppen to his mother and father, dated June 28, 1969.

Dear Mom and Dad,

I'm still on L.Z. Debbie. I've had K.P. twice so far and would just as soon be out in the field.

I just received your envelope with John Compton's letter, the bridge stuff, and the letter from you yesterday. It took two weeks to get here, but I'm glad to have it. It really sounds like John has it made. More power to him.

Yesterday we spent all day on a sweep through the valley below Debbie. They found an old beat up AK 47 rifle and two Viet Cong suspects. We (some men in the platoon, on orders from the local militia gestapo) burned several huts down. The militias (P.R.V.) are bullies and are used to interrogate the local citizens.

The food is better here, but there is much less free time. This is the first time in several days that I've had time to write letters. I plan to write six if I have time. There isn't much else to say so I'll sign off now. Write when you can and keep Kool-Aid coming.

Love Charlie

This is an excerpt from a letter that Lieutenant Baxter wrote to his parents on June 29, 1969.

We have had some good operations of late. The other day the platoon ran a search mission with PRU's an all Vietnamese outfit-a provincial forced which are about the best they have and 6 tracks & engineer demolition experts attached. We spent all day searching a small village and captured 5 VC and some AK-47's plus we blew up all the tunnels and bunkers. The PRU's did most of the work while my people & tracks provided security. All of this without firing a shot. It was just about our most successful mission . . . We're running missions with Vietnamese forces. Mostly we're here to give them confidence . . . but at least we're letting them run more of this war i.e. their war . . . lots of new people in my platoon this month—about 12 so my field strength is up a bit . . . most are

20 year old draftees from all over. Most of our losses have been normal rotation . . . many care packages of late . . . really don't need candy . . . a good package would be cookies maybe Fritos or peanuts, canned fruit, fruit juices . . . Well those are just some ideas that seem practical to a man in the boonies . . .

It was the end of June. We were still in the Rice Bowl and working with APCs from E Troop. The company moved in a staggered column formation with First Platoon to the front while the APCs took up the rear of the formation.

I was walking point and heard an explosion to my far left and rear. I hit the ground as a wheel and metal parts flew over the platoon as they ducked for cover. Crawling to a hedgerow for cover and concealment, I looked behind me and saw an APC burning. Everyone in the company took shelter and waited for the hail of weapons fire from the enemy. We waited several minutes and realized the APC had hit a booby trap and that it wasn't an ambush. I observed several officers, Captain Tyson one of them, in a group, talking. It wasn't long before Mike, Doc Windows, and another soldier approached the smoldering APC. Captain Tyson tasked them to remove the remains of the crew from the APC.

Once they'd completed removing the remains, I walked over to Mike and offered my canteen. He took several sips and handed my canteen back. We sat there, not talking. I never asked him what he did that day, and we never talked about it. I could tell it bothered Mike.

THE RICE BOWL

On July 1, we received word that Second Platoon had hit a booby trap that killed Sergeant Joseph Kelley and wounded another soldier. That night, First Platoon departed the FSB about 2130 hours for an all-night ambush. We set up our ambush position on the side of the mountain in an ant bed off Debbie; there was no enemy contact that night but plenty of ant bites. I got little sleep because I kept sliding downward on the steep incline and had to keep crawling back up to my position.

We returned the next morning about 0600 hours and settled in for sleep while the rest of Alpha Company, with the Cav unit, E Troop, worked the vicinity below us, the Rice Bowl.

The company ran into a U-shaped ambush and engaged an undetermined size enemy force. An APC hit a booby trap, and the company and E Troop had casualties within minutes—five Americans killed and seven wounded in action. One of the five killed was Sergeant Bobbie McCoy.

Lieutenant Colonel Ellis alerted Alpha Company's First Platoon, at 1520 hours, to reinforce its other two platoons. We gathered our gear, ensured we loaded up with ammo, and boarded the Huey helicopters, one squad per helicopter. We expected a hot landing zone. This was the same location where Sergeant Kelley of Third Platoon had been killed a day earlier. As we descended to the landing zone, we locked and loaded our weapons and prepared to jump off the Huey as soon as it was near the ground. We jumped to the ground before the skids touched and fanned out to secure the landing zone. We drew enemy small-arms fire as soon as our feet touched the ground.

Once on the ground, the platoon formed up, and we moved toward the enemy. Sergeant Stout directed me to move to the front and make sure no enemy soldiers were hiding in the hedgerows before the platoon moved through them. The hedgerows were about 10 feet wide and thick with trees, bamboo thickets, and clumps of brush. Jack Lanzer was behind me. He was five feet, nine inches and weighed 145 pounds, with red wavy hair; he was 20 years old. Dusty Rhoades followed Jack. He was 20 years old, medium build and height, and had dark hair. I moved forward, not seeing any enemy, but I still fired my M-16 in case an enemy soldier was hiding in the hedgerow, clearing one hedgerow after another, with the platoon following me. We were still receiving small-arms and machine-gun fire.

I looked back and to my right. Dusty and Lanzer broke through the hedgerow at a different place from me and stopped. Dusty turned and faced the hedgerow, and I heard him yell something but didn't understand what. As I moved toward Dusty, he pointed his M-60 and fired one round.

Dusty yelled, "My gun jammed—Gook in the hedgerow!"

Lanzer said, "I got him."

Lanzer pulled a grenade from his rucksack strap and pulled the pin. He took several steps backwards like a quarterback, released the handle, and threw the grenade into the hedgerow. Dusty and Lanzer hit the ground. Seeing Lanzer throw the grenade, I hit the ground and covered my head with my arms. The explosion vibrated the ground. Dusty got up and checked that the explosion had killed the enemy soldier hiding in the hedgerow. I jumped up and continued to move forward. I had to reload with a new magazine once as we moved through the hedgerows and again as we moved closer to the company.

Once we moved into the paddies, we linked up with the rest of the company, with second platoon to our left. Lieutenant Colonel Ellis positioned the APCs in a line behind the company. The platoons moved on-line from rice-paddy dike to rice-paddy dike, using the dikes for cover while the Cav unit provided covering fire with the .50 caliber machine gun and M-60 machine guns. We gave covering fire for the platoons as they moved forward, and they gave covering fire as we moved forward. I was sweating heavily, and my heart was pounding from the physical exertion and fear. Each time I moved to a dike, I lay as flat as I could, with my face against the ground for protection against the incoming rounds. The dry paddy dirt and my sweat covered my face with mud. Bullets thudded into the dike wall and sprayed dirt with zinging bullets over my head. I raised my M-16 above the dike with my head exposed and fired at the enemy positions. Then I jumped up with the rest of the platoon and ran forward to the next dike. We kept leapfrogging forward, firing at the enemy positions while receiving fire.

The enemy was still at a distance on a hill overlooking the paddies, and we couldn't gauge the effect of our fire and maneuver. We received mortar, machine-gun, and small-arms fire, bullets flying everywhere and explosions all around us! Captain Tyson called in air strikes to the hill, the source of the enemy fire. The jets came screaming over us and dropped the armament on the enemy's location. The F-4s flew so low we swore the ground shook beneath us. The enemy firing at us stopped. After the air strikes, we received orders to move toward the hill.

First Platoon was the lead platoon, and I was the point man. Lieutenant Baxter said, "Let's move out," and I stood there waiting.

The Lieutenant asked, "Haynie, why are you waiting?"

I replied, "I am waiting for the tracks to move to the front, Sir."

The Lieutenant, in an impatient tone, said, "We walk point, not the tracks."

I said, "OK, sir" and moved out toward the hill.

I thought it best if the tracks took the lead; that's how we'd done it in training. On the hill, we found enemy dead and blood trails. The enemy had fled. We found enemy dead in the hedgerows we'd cleared earlier. There were 22 enemy soldiers killed that day.

We formed up and waited for the Hueys to pick us up and fly back to Debbie. First Platoon was the last platoon to leave, as usual. We secured the landing zone for the company. After we loaded and flew back to Debbie, we landed on the helicopter pad, jumped off, and headed to our bunkers tired, hungry, and thirsty. We dropped our gear off, cleaned up, and headed to the mess hall for a hot meal. I met Mike at the mess hall, and we talked about the events of the day. After the meal, we got a well-deserved rest.

Not much later, Sergeant Stout left the platoon for a rear job, and Dennis Stout left the platoon for Hawaii; the Army decided to enforce the "no-brothers-in-a-combat-zone" rule. Joe Mitchell became the first squad leader, a nice guy with wavy blond hair, married, and 20 years old. Joe had no leadership training, and it was common for someone to be given a leadership position with the soldiers (friends) they served, a buddy one day and the boss the next. Some handled it, and others didn't.

This is an excerpt from a letter that Charlie Deppen wrote to his parents on July 3, 1969.

Dear Mom & Dad,

First of all I want to thank you for the Kool-Aid you send me. It hits the spot. Keep mixing them up, since although I like cherry and grape best, the variety is good.

. . . Almost every four or five days we get an SP pack with cigarettes, lots of candy, writing material and toilet articles. The candy is the type that keeps well in this climate . . .

. . . When we clean up in the villes we use their wells and well water to wash with. Our steel helmets serve as a wash basin to shave in.

All in all, the times over here not "all" bad, and it may not be quite as bad over here as you think it is. It's not that every day is like a living hell, it's just that certain times and certain things are bad or uncomfortable. I have yet to have a single shot fired at me personally, as far as I know.

I'd had KP four times since we've been here. If this keeps up I won't be too sorry to leave.

Lately we have been working with armored personnel carriers (APCs). They are full tracks and mount two M60 machineguns and one 50 cal. machinegun. We either walk beside them or ride four or five on the top. It sure beats walking!

Well, that's it for now. Keep the bridge columns and letters coming. . . .

Love Charlie

GOING TO SECOND SQUAD

I'd approached Lieutenant Baxter several weeks earlier to explain that I wanted to move to second squad. Mike and I had developed a good friendship since we'd arrived at the platoon and thought it great if we could be in the same squad. I made friends in first squad. But I didn't hit it off as well with anyone as I did with Mike. Lieutenant Baxter said he would see what he could do. I knew it was a strange request, but I figured, "What the hell?" and asked.

Not long after Joe became the squad leader, Lieutenant Baxter agreed to move Chuck Council to first squad and me to second squad. Chuck was from Oregon, losing his hair, and older than most of us; he was a likeable person and always had a big smile. Chuck gathered up his gear and moved over to first squad with no complaints. Once with first squad, Dusty Rhoades nicknamed Chuck "Pops" because he was the old guy in the squad at 23 years old.

Jerry Ofstedahl introduced himself as the Squad Leader. Jerry was 20 years old; he was from California and had been with the platoon since December 1968. By reputation he was a good and fair leader. I told him thanks for taking me and that I would give him no reason to doubt his decision.

This is an excerpt from a letter that Lieutenant Baxter wrote to his parents on July 3 and 5, 1969.

> . . . Despite of talks of withdrawal, etc., the war goes on and Alpha Company has seen her share of late. At least being on a fire base we can relax a little more, get cleaned up daily instead of being in the field all the time. I often wonder how this thing i.e. the war is changing me-does it show in my letters. I know I hate the NVA (do I really? Or do I just seem to?) And we give them no quarter. Maybe it's the sense of survival with a little eye for an eye thrown in. I know all this is not nice to write about but I feel I must. In any event I don't look at this as job as some do but an ordeal to be endured. . . .
>
> . . . Tomorrow we leave LZ Debbie . . .to a new area . . . we're still not sure where yet. Replacements have filled my platoon to its highest strength yet-27. But this creates problems because there are so many green ones . . ..I've been a little busier and haven't written that much . . . not too much to write about . . . hot but we are getting more rain. . . .

Figure 17 John "Mississippi" DeLoach next to 105mm. Photo provided by John DeLoach.

Figure 18 Warren McVey and Bruce Tufts on right (KIA June 14, 1969). Photo provided by Chuck Council.

Figure 19 Dennis Rowe (WIA June 14, 1969.) with M60 machine gun. Photo provided by Chuck Council.

Figure 20 Nick VanDyke (WIA June 14, 1969) and Jerry Ofstedahl on right (KIA August 13, 1969) on break. Photo provided by Bruce Nugget.

Figure 21 FSB Debbie/ Thunder with view of Rice Bowl, top of frame. Photo provided by Carl Bjelland.

Figure 22 Glyn Haynie and Mike Dankert on right getting water from well. Photo provided by Glyn Haynie.

CHAPTER 5

THE HILL

BUILDING A FIREBASE

On July 6, the company loaded on Chinook helicopters and departed FSB Debbie, heading to FSB Bronco. The Brigade FSB was a good break. Captain Tyson briefed the entire company on our new mission and AO. The Battalion Commander assigned Alpha Company to build a fire support base in Quang Ngai Valley.

A fire support base was a forward base with a company of infantry for security. It provides fire support with 81mm and 4.2-inch mortars and artillery for the units working the AO around the FSB. The work was to be a joint effort between our battalion, 11th Brigade's 3rd/1st, and the 4th ARVN regiment.

The name of the new Fire Support Base was to be 4-11, recognizing that cooperative effort. Alpha Company led a large task force building the FSB. The American soldiers did the actual building while the ARVNs provided security. Lieutenant Colonel Ellis scheduled us to leave the morning of July 8th. We spent the next day preparing for our new mission.

The morning of July 8, our platoon, in a column of two's, entered the rear of the Chinook helicopter, and the Chinook lifted off to take us to secure the new firebase location on a hill seven miles west of Quang Ngai City. The Chinook landed without receiving enemy fire, and we exited through the rear door as soon as it dropped. We then moved up the hill and encountered many mines and booby traps along the crest of the hill. The company deployed a minesweeping device, manned by Sergeant Owens, and got on line to sweep the hill for booby traps. We found booby-trapped grenades, 2.75-inch rockets, and a canister full of napalm with a firing device planted in the ground.

Captain Tyson erected a sign on top of the hill that named the hill Fire Support Base Kelley-McCoy. Kelley and McCoy were two NCOs killed one day apart in the Rice Bowl a week earlier. However, the name 4-11 became the official name of the firebase. The companies would take turns building the FSB. Alpha Company took the first 30-day rotation while the other companies patrolled the new AO along with the ARVNs. This "Hill" soon defined our platoon and the AO we patrolled.

The Hill, 50 meters high, had a commanding view of the entire AO to the river and the mountains. The Hill was barren, with worn trails and areas of knee-high grass. Below the Hill was a cleared field surrounding the Hill 100 meters in depth with an occasional strand of bamboo. In no time, engineers removed the bamboo.

East, half a klick from the Hill, was an old foundation of a French fort, a concrete bunker, and an airfield barely visible in the ground. We thought it strange that the fort wasn't on the Hill. That was a bad omen to us! We often wondered if the French held this position or were defeated and had to leave before the end of their war.

First Platoon covered the east side and parts of the Hill's south side. I had never seen so many different units and types of equipment in one location. There were combat engineer platoons with bulldozers to build the Hill and clear the vicinity below the Hill, E Troop Cavalry APCs for protection, and artillery for fire support. The bulldozers worked through the day digging bunker positions, and engineers erected the bunker frames.

The platoon had been very busy since our arrival. We worked during the day and fought at night. We worked seven days a week from sunrise to dusk. The Division and Brigade Information Offices covered the events that occurred on the Hill, including our arrival to the Hill.

We needed to fill thousands of sandbags to protect our bunkers. Along with building the bunkers, we installed concertina wire. This was barbed wire, or razor wire, in large coils forming a barrier around the Hill. The platoon laid two strands of rolled concertina wire and the third strand on top of the first two.

The first bunker we prepared was a culvert cut in half, three feet high and six to eight feet long. We placed it in a position behind the bunker location. We sandbagged the top and sides three sandbags deep. This was our protection until the bunker could be built. Most evenings around 1900 hours we heard the "thump, thump, thump" of enemy-fired mortar rounds, which gave us less than 10 seconds to find cover. We received three or four mortar rounds nearly every night. We learned to quit work before 1900 hours and head to our culvert bunker for cover. Mike, John Meyer, and I always thought we could be in the line of fire because the Company CP was right behind us. It was at a higher elevation, with many antennas sticking up, and was an obvious target for the enemy.

We installed trip flares and claymore mines to the front of our positions. We hung Coke and beer cans with rocks inside from the concertina wire for early warning. When the enemy would try to crawl through the wire, it jiggled it, and the can rattled, signaling us that NVA or VC were trying to breach the perimeter. Several nights we took patrols outside the Hill perimeter to set up an ambush site. Checking our claymore mines, we occasionally found them turned around facing us—proof that we weren't alone and that we'd had visitors in the night.

We spent nights pulling two-hour guard shifts, while we weren't on alert, which was every night the first week. There was enemy contact six of our first seven nights on the Hill; nightly mortar rounds, rockets, and sapper attacks. The worst was the sapper attack, where enemy soldiers penetrated our defenses and threw a satchel charge, explosives, into a position. The enemy knew where our positions were. Lieutenant Baxter told us no US forces had patrolled the AO for a long time, so we expected a large NVA/VC presence.

On July 10, about 2230 hours, we endured the tail-end of Typhoon Tess that delivered more than six inches of rain along with heavy winds. That night was cold and wet. John, Mike, and I huddled in our small shelter, each of us wrapped in a poncho liner and poncho over the liner to stay warm and dry, but with little success. Mike and I lay on the wet ground with our backs touching to keep each other warm. The wind howled and pelted our shelter with heavy rain. The water flowed in a steady stream underneath us through the shelter. We had nowhere else to go, so we remained in the shelter trapped like wet rats. We hoped there wouldn't be an attack that night! Early the next morning, at 0130 hours, the perimeter received four or five RPG rounds that hit nothing. We ignored the RPG rounds and stayed hunkered in the shelter.

The next morning we got up at sunrise and discovered deep mud covering the Hill. We were soaking wet, cold, and covered in mud. Later that morning, Second Platoon checked their perimeter wire and reported the wire cut. I guessed the NVA didn't get the weather warning. Although it took days for everything to dry out, we continued to work on the construction.

The next day at 2100 hours, Mike and I sat at our position talking and drinking a Coke, with John on guard duty. I was about to say I was ready for bed, when, out of nowhere, we heard songs playing from the jungle 800 meters away. Everyone on the Hill got quiet. The three songs played were "Where Have All the Flowers Gone?" by Peter, Paul and Mary, "Oh, Susannah" by James Taylor and "North to Alaska" by Johnny Horton. The sound quality was good. Then the broadcast changed to someone speaking in excellent English asking us why we were fighting in Vietnam. He told us to surrender, come over to their side, or get wiped out. Mike and I were speechless. It was unnerving! We gave our response; our artillery opened fire toward the music and voice, which made us duck for cover. They fired more than 100 artillery rounds to silence the NVA. Once the artillery ceased firing and through the rising smoke and dust, the voice came back and taunted us for our poor marksmanship. That pissed off Mike and me. We'd never seen this tactic used. It made us think a bigger force than we had expected might be out there. We would receive the same broadcast a day or two later (see Appendix E).

Later that night, about 2220 hours, the company spotted five VC about 100 meters from the wire. The positions opened up with small-arms fire and 81mm mortar fire. The VC fled. Ten minutes later, several bunker positions reported 15 NVA in the wire. Units on the Hill opened fire again with .50 caliber machine guns, 81mm mortars, artillery, and small-arms fire, and the enemy fled. The next morning we found no bodies.

The firebase took shape after the first week. The engineers had dug out the bunker positions and were getting ready to install the bunker shells. Each day since we'd arrived, with instructions from the combat engineers, we pounded in fence posts and strung concertina wire between the posts in front of the platoon positions. It had taken the company days to circle the Hill with concertina wire. At the end of each day, no matter where I was going, I held my hand out in front of my body so as not to walk into the wire; I had strung so much concertina wire, I thought I was seeing the wire in front of me with every step I took.

This is a letter from Charlie Deppen to his mother, father, brother, and sister, dated July 12, 1969.

Dear Mom, Dad, David and Nancy,

I am writing this letter to the four of you to save time and also because I'm short of writing material. I should get more in an SP pack any day now.

For the last five days we have been building a fire base about two miles west of Quang Ngai. The first day we cleared and occupied the hill. Next we laid two strands of rolled barbed wire and

WHEN I TURNED NINETEEN

another on top. This took the second and third days. The last two days we worked on a small bunker type fighting position. They really keep us busy. Two nights ago it rained so hard and long that we had a lake in our primary guard and sleeping positions. Everyone on the hill was wet and cold (yes cold). Luckily we now have overhead cover and the weather is somewhat better.

Wish me luck and put a hex on the Dinks.

Love Charlie

There were nights the company had a "mad minute." There was a specific time at night or early morning the company gave instructions that every position and weapon fire for one minute to the front of their position. It looked and sounded as if the world was ending from the explosions, tracer rounds, and the sounds of different weapons. After one minute it got eerily quiet because everyone ceased firing at the same time. The reasoning was this tactic helped in discouraging the enemy from attacking. It allowed everyone to fire their weapons and to check if the weapon was functioning correctly. Hopefully, the enemy was unaware of the exact time we started the "mad minute."

This is an excerpt from a letter that Lieutenant Baxter wrote to his parents and sister on July 13, 1969.

We're now building the new fire base some 10km due west of Quang Ngai City. A fire support base is a forward base that gives infantry fire support from 81&4.2 mortars and 104 & 155mm artillery.

We have about a two hundred man task force headed by our company building this thing. We also have an ARVN battalion pulling security for us. Despite all this the VC & NVA have propaganda teams trying to get us to surrender-they have . . .loudspeakers blaring away in the early evening.

It is really quite a project: our company, two engineer platoons, 9 armored personnel carriers . . ..two bulldozers working all day

84

digging bunkers . . . Right now we are working on the 97,000
sandbags that are needed for the project . . .On top of that we
were hit by the backend of a typhoon . . . 6+" of rain . . . made for a
miserable night as well as tons of mud the next day . . . On a bright
note I have an in-country R&R to DaNang on the 27th.

Once we got on the Hill, Captain Tyson started a beard-growing
contest that lasted a week. Once the contest ended, Captain Tyson passed
the order that everyone shave. One evening Mike and I were sitting
outside Lieutenant Baxter's bunker talking. I was enjoying a cigarette,
and Lieutenant Baxter was puffing on one of his big cigars. Mike never
smoked. Being on a firebase or stand-down was the only time Lieutenant
Baxter smoked cigars. I don't remember him smoking in the field.

This particular evening Captain Tyson walked around the bunker
line and stopped at the bunker to talk to Lieutenant Baxter. He looked at
me and in an angry voice asked Lieutenant Baxter, "Why hasn't Haynie
shaved?" Lieutenant Baxter and everyone else laughed, but Captain
Tyson didn't see the humor.

Lieutenant Baxter stated, "Sir, Haynie has not shaved since he has
been here." And everyone laughed again.

Now, in my defense, I had a battery-operated Norelco shaver my
mother had given me as a going-away present, and I used it weekly to
remove any peach fuzz! Captain Tyson still didn't see the humor, but he
shook his head and walked away. Lieutenant Baxter suggested that I shave.

Each night Mike and I pulled guard duty together, sitting back to
back; one could nap and wake the other if he felt sleepy. We took off
our gear and helmets while pulling guard; the helmet got heavy after
wearing it during the day. Our guard position was on top of the dirt
mound the engineers had created digging the position for the bunker.
One night I was awake as Mike slept, and I noticed extra fence posts in
the fence line. I counted and recounted the posts and figured there were
two extra posts. I woke Mike and had him verify the extra posts, which
he did. We shouted at the same time, "Gooks in the wire."

We opened fire at the fence line toward the "extra post." Next came small-arms fire and explosions. Then in no time, the whole company opened fire on the perimeter of the Hill.

The platoon sergeant, Staff Sergeant Swindle, came running up and shouted, "What is going on?"

Mike responded, "Gooks in the wire!"

Staff Sergeant Swindle yelled, "Get your helmets on," and he went back to tell Lieutenant Baxter what was happening.

Staff Sergeant Swindle was in his 30s and a "lifer," a career soldier, and I respected him for that. You didn't find too many career soldiers in the field leading the young troops; we had 19- or 20-year-olds as the leaders. Most lifer NCOs were in the rear with a job that didn't involve leading soldiers.

The next morning we found no bodies at the fence post locations. This wasn't unusual because the VC dragged away their dead.

While building the firebase, we had two or three ARVN 4-11 Battalion soldiers stay at our position at night, as did the other bunker positions. It didn't take long for personal items to go missing throughout the company. We had the same ARVNs stay at our position, and we tried to communicate using broken English, broken Vietnamese, and sign language. One ARVN soldier liked my watch, but I had no interest in trading, selling, or giving it away. It stayed on my wrist any time they were there.

One evening as we prepared our evening meal, the ARVN soldiers brought their meal and brought enough for Mike, John, and me. It was a stew with chunks of meat, rice, potatoes, and other, unidentifiable, ingredients. The ARVN said the meat was beef. Yeah, right. To this day, Mike and I believe we had dog meat that night. The meal tasted different and too spicy for me.

SAPPERS IN THE PERIMETER JULY 14

We finished our dinner meal and enjoyed an evening of rest by our bunker shell. The thought of sandbagging for hours on end to fortify our bunker didn't sound appealing. As it neared dusk, we moved to our sandbagged culvert for cover from the nightly mortar and rocket attacks. Sure enough, at 1900 hours, we heard the "thump, thump, thump" of five or six mortar rounds being fired. The incoming rounds missed any bunkers or areas where soldiers were taking shelter. When the nightly mortar attack ended, we finished talking and moving around and got ready to rest for the night.

Early the next morning, at 0100 hours, Third Platoon observed five VC near/in their perimeter wire. A trip flare went off, and one of Third Platoon's bunkers set off a claymore, but they didn't know if they'd killed the intruder. They reported four VC outside the wire and one inside the wire. Ten minutes later, sappers made it through the wire and hit the Third Platoon positions. Third platoon laid down intensive automatic-weapons and rifle fire to kill and repel the enemy. The rest of the positions from around the hill, including ours, moved to our fighting positions, opened fire, and continued firing for 10 minutes. Then it got quiet for several minutes. Third platoon killed one VC/NVA who'd gotten inside the perimeter in front of their positions. Minutes later we heard the crack of M-16 and AK-47 weapons firing on the opposite side of the hill near the Third Platoon positions again.

Sergeant Techmeir from the Third Platoon took a patrol outside the wire to pursue the sappers. They believed four VC/NVA were still outside the wire. He found a three-foot hole cut in the wire. Once they'd moved outside the wire, the enemy ambushed the patrol and killed Sergeant Techmeir. The rest of the patrol carried him back to the platoon position. Once the patrol got back inside and at their bunkers, we opened fire again. Third Platoon reported that they'd killed another VC/NVA. We secured the perimeter. Captain Tyson didn't call in a dust-off for Sergeant Techmeir until the next morning.

With little sleep, we spent most of the day checking our positions, claymore mines, and trip flares, and cleaning our weapons. We double-checked the wire in front of our position for any holes. Everyone remained on edge from the early-morning attack. We were not feeling as secure now. As the sun dropped, those not on guard duty tried to get rest.

Dusty, Ramos, Reynolds, and Okino were at the bunker on the south side of the hill. It was getting late. Dusty noticed that Ramos was acting strangely—nothing he could name, just gut instinct, but different from the norm. Reynolds listened to a tape from his wife and continued to replay it over and over again. Reynolds was new, an FNG assigned to the platoon three weeks previous. Ryan Okino sat on the hillside behind the bunker, enjoying the evening. Chuck Council was in the hospital at Duc Pho with jungle rot on his leg and assigned to the same bunker.

Before dark Dusty went to the front of his bunker to set the trip flares; he was the expert for his bunker position. Dusty was quiet but friendly and hailed from the western plains of Nebraska, where he was a deadly shot against prairie dogs and jackrabbits on his father's ranch. He set the trip flares and found no problems with the front of the position.

A trip flare illuminated the front of the bunker position at 2130 hours. Dusty yelled for Ramos and Reynolds to throw a grenade to the front and fire at any movement. Dusty picked up his M-16 and stepped around the corner of the bunker, ready to fire at an enemy soldier's outline in the darkness. Suddenly there was a bright orange and white light, with no accompanying sound, which at once made him disoriented and confused. In a short time, Dusty appeared to know of his surroundings and fired his M-16 toward the fence line until he passed out. As he came to, Doc Windows and Okino tried to discover where his wounds were. Doc Windows had a flashlight with a red lens, and every time he pointed at a different part of Dusty's body, he said "Oh shit, oh shit, oh shit" thinking he'd found a wound. Eventually Doc Windows found several long and deep shrapnel wounds from the satchel charge explosion in Dusty's back and right hand.

Explosions and automatic weapons fire startled the platoon from sleep. A sapper had made it through the perimeter and thrown a satchel charge into the bunker, killing Juan Ramos and Eldon Reynolds. Critically wounded was Dusty Rhoades. The company received small-arms fire, and chi-com grenades exploded from the south, west and east. Captain Tyson requested flare ships and gunships from Chu Lai for support of the Hill. Until the support arrived, the company provided illumination with 4.2 mortars and suppressive fire with 81mm mortars and 105mm artillery.

Dusty remembered Doc Windows and Okino picking him up, one on each side, because his legs didn't work. He told Doc Windows he felt no pain. He tried to figure out why he couldn't walk. They carried Dusty up the hill to an APC behind the bunker. The APC commander dropped the door, and Doc Windows and Okino put Dusty inside the APC with another soldier.

The soldier inside repeated to Dusty, "Please don't get sick" over and over again; he appeared scared. Dusty kept telling the scared soldier, "I will not get sick." He felt confused about what was going on around him as gunships fired, and automatic and small arms fired around the Hill.

First Platoon soon opened fire on the perimeter to kill or discourage any other sappers from getting to our positions. The rest of the company fired automatic weapons and rifle fire to the front of their positions. The flare ships and gunships arrived, and we stopped firing. They remained until 2230 hours that night. The flare ships would light up the night sky as if sunlight was filtering through the clouds, mixing light and shadows, which made visibility of the perimeter possible. The gunship fired its mini-guns around the Hill's perimeter to keep the enemy back.

Captain Tyson called for a dust-off at 2140 hours. Other platoon members removed Reynolds and Ramos from the bunker, carried them to the helicopter landing pad, and covered them with ponchos. At 2210 hours the dust-off landed, and two soldiers carried Dusty to the dust-off on a litter and placed him on the top row; they placed Ramos and Reynolds on the bottom, below Dusty. They loaded the last body, and the dust-off took off, heading to the Division Hospital at Chu Lai while the company gave covering fire. After they were airborne, Dusty reached downward and shook Ramos by the boots, asking if he was OK. Ramos didn't respond.

Dusty grabbed the crew chief and asked, "These are my buddies. What the hell is happening?"

The crew chief didn't respond to Dusty's question and said, "Don't go into shock; don't go into shock."

Dusty lay back, thinking, *What the hell is this guy talking about?* The next thing he knew, they were landing in Chu Lai. They removed Ramos and Reynolds first and took them in a different direction than they took Dusty. They wheeled Dusty into a secure bunker position, and he still had no pain. This was where his descent into hell began.

It was after midnight, and there was no enemy to engage; the enemy had disappeared into the darkness. The platoon got ready for much-needed sleep.

Talking with Ryan Okino later the next day, he said that he'd observed a German Shepherd dog approaching the bunker carrying an object. He claimed the dog, not a sapper, dropped the grenade or satchel charge into the bunker.

This is a letter that Chuck Council wrote to Dusty Rhoades after learning of the sapper attack on his bunker while in the hospital at Duc Pho.

Dear Dusty,

It's mid July 1969. The heat outside is stifling. I am in the Brigade hospital back in Duc Pho recovering from an injury to my leg. The hospital staff has an extensive collection of musical tapes—anything you want to hear as long as it is Roy Orbison's Greatest Hits. Roy Orbison over and over and over again. I'm so sick of Roy Orbison I could throw up. With each passing day, I increasingly long to return to the bush just to escape the tyranny of Roy Orbison.

Then one day Rebel comes to visit me. He brings the news. My squad's position on Hill 411 was hit a couple of nights ago by enemy sappers. Ramos and Reynolds were killed. Dusty was shot up badly and was evacuated out by chopper. Status unknown. The only survivor is Okino. Shock waves roll over me like a runaway locomotive. I don't know whether it's day or night. I should have been there, but I was not. I'm here in the hospital. I get up out of my bed and hobble slowly over to the cooler to get a drink of water. A Roy Orbison song is playing softly on the stereo. Chuck

DUSTY'S ROAD TO RECOVERY BY TIMOTHY "DUSTY" RHOADES

At the Chu Lai hospital a huge corpsman cut off my clothes, and that pissed me off because there were female nurses there and I didn't want to be naked in front of them. Before I knew it, he had me naked from the waist down. The corpsman got out a plastic container and pulled a tube out of it and I asked him "What the hell are you doing?" The corpsman replied "I'm going to put this in your penis" and I said "Like the hell you are." Within a few minutes and a struggle I had a tube in my dick. He pulled out another tube and plastic container, and I asked him "What are you going to do with that?" And he replied "Putting it up your nose." I said "Like hell it is" and after a struggle I had a tube in my nose. Now I am naked with a tube coming out of my nose and a tube coming out of my dick. There are female nurses standing right in front of me and I felt embarrassed. They wheeled me to a black cold table for x-rays and the last thing I heard was "Don't get sick" as I puked and passed out.

I woke up, several days later and still at the hospital in Chu Lai. I had an intravenous fluid drip (IV) in my arm and lived off the fluids from the IV for an undetermined number of days. I drifted into sleep due to the pain medication and awaken from the pain. A never-ending cycle. Awake I looked at the tube running from my nose to a machine and saw something green running from my nose to a container. I had multiple wounds, left side of my back and right wrist. The doctor sliced me open from the sternum to below the beltline during the operation to repair my wounds. They bandaged most of my wounds but they didn't stitch them so they could drain. It hurt like hell every time they changed my bandages.

I was in a haze as time passed between dressing changes, medication, painkillers and other medical needs. One evening as I lay awake confined to my bed a nurse asked if I wanted to call home to my parents. I said yes. I gave the nurse the phone number, and she said they would dial the number through a Military Auxiliary Radio System (MARS). A nurse wheeled me to the nurse's station and handed me a telephone handset. They gave me instructions to say the word "over" after completing what you are saying. The person you talked to did the same. This technique determined who talked and who listened.

Overwhelmed with emotions they dialed my mother and father phone number. My mother answered, and I told her I was fine but not sure she believed me and my father picked up and asked "What was going on and where are you? Over" I said "I am on R & R over." I didn't want to worry them. My father asked right away wasn't it too early to be on R & R. He was in WW II and familiar with how the Army operates. I told him everything was OK and not to worry I wanted to say hello. That ended our telephone call.

I was in the Chu Lai hospital for five days and then transferred to Cam Ranh Bay. While in the Chu Lai hospital I learned the nurses were wonderful, and you never wanted to look bad in their eyes because there were other guys you thought had wounds worse than you.

Once I arrived to the Cam Ranh Bay hospital, the doctors did a quick triage and moved me to a hospital bed. The only thing I remember was watching the weather girl on television. She wore a short skirt, and I thought what the hell? Somewhere between Chu Lai and Cam Ranh Bay one of the Stout brothers stopped by and asked what happened and how was I doing. I remember little of the brief visit.

The doctor told me "You have a million-dollar wound and you're going home" which I didn't understand what he said. I remember little of the trip from Cam Ranh Bay to Japan. After two days in Japan the nurse removed my catheter and I remember having to pee. I stood there peeing as if it would never stop. As I peed three guys peed and left. I know it's hard to understand, but I thought it amazing. I can pee on my own again and with a full stream. After I went back to my bed, the doctors selected many wounded to return to the states. I was one of them.

I remember landing in Alaska and the General of the base greeted us. The doors swung open, and he offered everyone a steak dinner. Most soldiers on the plane were hooked to IVs and catheters and couldn't eat a steak dinner much less go to the mess hall. Someone from the back yelled "Close the damn door we are freezing." I felt sorry for the General because he didn't know the passengers on the plane held wounded soldiers that couldn't leave the plane or eat a meal.

The next stop was Scott Air Force Base, Illinois. I was one of the first unloaded from the plane and loaded onto a military bus converted for stretchers. There was a beautiful woman helping the soldiers and trying to make us more comfortable. The soldier lying next to me and I referenced the sexual acts we would do with her if given the opportunity. Unfortunately, the other nurses overheard our conversation and now the nurses wanted nothing to do with us but the oldest nurse that probably served in WW II. It was the same old nurse that got me for my phone call home.

I arrived at the Army Hospital at Fort Riley Kansas and spent one week in an open ward with many wounded soldiers. It was during this time I received a box with my belongings. My airborne boots and dog tags was what I received. During my recovery I never forgot Ramos or Reynolds and often wondered what and why it happened. The pain of losing my friends started on the Hill and never ended. In August I asked a candy striper to write two letters to Chuck and the platoon. I told them I was in the states and doing fine and asked how first squad and the platoon was doing. I missed everyone. The nurses told me to get ready for a move to the Fort Irwin Hospital.

Once arriving at the hospital at Fort Irwin they placed me on the third floor and in a special bed. The guy to the right of me was a combat infantry veteran having served one year in Vietnam. In Vietnam he never received a scratch. A car accident put him here not long after returning home with both arms and legs in traction.

The nurse came in the room and bent over my bed checking my wounds and explaining my injuries, at that point the soldier next to me pushed her on the ass. She fell on me screaming and then I screamed. She went to the soldier's bed and pulled on the sandbags of his traction. He would never do that again after the pain he experienced from the change to his traction.

I became discouraged when I didn't receive a letter from the platoon responding to the two letters I wrote. I felt everybody blamed me for what happened that night. This haunted me for many years, in my sleep, and my waking hours and it never stopped.

I was on a ward with twenty to forty other people who had lost everything from their sight to legs and arms. The girlfriend's, fiancée's and wives visited their loved ones on Friday nights. After the visit we all knew, except for the poor guy being visited, that they were never coming back. I was there for many Dear John letters and seeing attorneys serving divorce papers. The wives couldn't handle what they saw. My wounded comrade's pain went deep, deeper than you can ever imagine. The pain of no response from the platoon had the same impact on me.

On July 15, Charlie Company reported finding an NVA hospital and a Basic Training center 15 klicks from the firebase. They called in an airstrike and destroyed both. The hospital complex had one hooch destroyed, eight hooches damaged, and one bunker destroyed. They found wooden chi-coms and a tank obstacle course at the suspected Basic Training center.

A dust-off landed, at 1845 hours, to pick up Doc Windows because of smoke inflammation and respiratory impairment; he was flown to the Chu Lai hospital. He would not return to the platoon. Now the platoon was without a medic.

The next day at 0230, Shadow opened fire on the Hill with its mini-guns. We all woke and sought better protection from the incoming rounds and wondered what the hell is happening! Shadow was a C-130 decked out with mini-guns and plenty of firepower. The ARVNs called in the fire mission on the Hill. Captain Tyson contacted the ARVN commander to cease fire. Damn ARVNs—they're supposed to be on our side!

LIVING ON THE HILL

Building the firebase was hard and boring work, but we had comforts not available in the field. We had a mess hall that provided three hot cooked meals a day, ice-cold drinks, and sometimes snacks while on guard duty. There were cold showers available every day. For grunts, we could stay clean. The platoon received clean clothes more often while building the firebase, and then there were the outhouses (shitters) that we used. We didn't have to wander off the trail to take a shit. We slept in a bunker with protection above and around us and even took our boots and helmets off to sleep. The platoon had plenty of protection with the artillery, APCs, and other fixed-gun positions. With the luxury comes a price because we had to pull KP, police call, and shit-burning details. Sometimes we wanted to leave the firebase for the field despite the luxury the firebase offered. We wanted more freedom over the confinement and boredom of living on the firebase. The continued alerts at night and working on the bunkers during the hottest part of the day caused tension and frustration.

Mike, John, and I finished sandbagging the bunker. Mike laid the last sandbag on the roof of the bunker in the early evening, and we decided to sit back, rest, and enjoy a Coke. As young guys do, we talked smack to each other and used the roof of the bunker as a wrestling ring. We met in the center of the "ring" and grappled to get the best takedown position. I had a good-enough position to bring Mike to the mat and went for the pin and the win (now if Mike was telling this story, I was the one getting pinned). At that moment we heard a loud *swoosh* sound right over our heads. A 75mm round exploded hitting the west side of the Hill. We crawled to the end of the roof, lowered ourselves to the ground, and got inside the bunker for cover. Once safe, we laughed and claimed the other lucky that the NVA had saved them.

We relaxed more on the Hill. We had time to talk. This was the '60s, and the Vietnam War was controversial. There were plenty of topics to discuss. John Meyer and Mike were avid music fans, and they talked of different groups and singers. I was never into music and didn't stay current.

One day Meyer asked, "Haynie have you heard the songs 'Lady Lady Lay' or 'Country Pie'?"

I replied, "No, Meyer. I have not."

He replied, "Bob Dylan wrote and sang the songs. Have you heard of him?"

I said, "No. Who is Bob Dylan?"

Meyer got red in the face and didn't believe I didn't know Dylan. This became a standard dialog and joke between John Meyer and me. I know who he was now!

Another benefit to being on the Hill the company allowed soldiers to go back to the brigade firebase, Bronco (in Duc Pho), for what I called the "royal treatment." One morning Lieutenant Baxter selected Alabama (Ray Hamilton) and me to return to Bronco on the battalion supply chopper. Ray was the M-60 gunner and from Alabama, married, 20 years old, quiet, and religious. We got along well.

We gathered our weapons and ammo, jumped into the Huey, and sat on the floor with our legs dangling out over the skids. The Huey lifted and banked as it moved away from the Hill. After a short ride, we landed on the helicopter pad at Bronco, jumped out, and walked to the company headquarters. First Sergeant Malpica greeted us as we entered through the screen door. He sent us to supply for clean uniforms (that fit) and any other clothing we might need.

Next we went to the bathhouse with a line of soldiers awaiting their turns. We checked in with the hostess and started our wait. Within minutes, the hostess directed us to our private rooms. Here I received a steam bath—bathed and massaged by a young Vietnamese woman. After our relaxing morning, Alabama said, "I haven't felt this clean and relaxed in many months," and I agreed. We paid three dollars MPC and left.

We dropped off our old, dirty uniforms at supply and went to the mess hall for lunch. The food tasted better than our mess hall on the Hill; we had steak for lunch! Then we went to the helicopter pad and waited for the Huey ride home. Within 15 minutes the helicopter landed, supply soldiers loaded ammunition and supplies, and we lifted off and headed back to the Hill. Once we got back to the squad, Alabama and I talked of the great time we had and made sure everyone was sufficiently envious of our trip.

Mike and I got up early on July 19, went to the mess hall, and had our usual breakfast meal of eggs, bacon, potatoes, and toast. As we sat at the table eating, I remembered that it was his 20th birthday. I told Mike happy birthday and that I was glad he'd made it another year. Mike was, too! After breakfast we walked back to the bunker to continue to fill and place sandbags on and around the bunker. Keeping the bunker maintained was a never-ending job.

It turned out to be another uneventful day with us working on the bunker, checking trip flares, and claymore mines; John Meyer attached several more Coke cans, with rocks on the inside, to the concertina wire in front of our position. We worked on the inside of the bunker to organize and create as much living space as possible. Our position was as ready as it could be for nightfall.

Mike and I moved outside the bunker for the first guard shift of the night and took up our positions, sitting next to each other, facing the concertina wire to our front. Visibility was better outside the bunker. I got out two cans of pound cake, opened both, and handed one to Mike. I again told him happy birthday and that this was his birthday cake. No candles because we didn't want the light to give away our position. As we ate the pound cake and sipped on unsweetened Kool-Aid, Mike remarked how America had launched Apollo 11 several days previous to go to the moon—but we couldn't end a damn war. I agreed with that statement! Mike's birthday ended with no interruption from the enemy, so he had a happy birthday.

On July 22, we learned of Neil Armstrong walking on the moon. We acknowledged the feat, but there were no loud shouts of triumph from the platoon. I know most were thinking, *The hell with the moon—end the war and get us home!*

This is an excerpt from a letter that Lieutenant Baxter wrote to his parents and sister on July 21, 1969.

"We completed two weeks of working on FSB Kelley-McCoy. Work has been going slow due to weather and lack of materials . . . things have quieted considerably . . . Thanks for the books maybe I'll get to read a few now that life is a little more settled . . . Un popped popcorn is fine-we do have fire over here. Met a Lt in Bn from Brooksville a '67 UF grad. My platoon has lost strength again—a combination of some getting jobs in the rear and casualties. Both my RTO' got jobs in the rear-so lots of training for the new ones. The other had been with me all along and I depended on them quite a bit."

SETTING UP AN AMBUSH

It was late July, and we were still on the Hill, building Fire Support Base 4-11. We not only provided security for the Hill while building the firebase, but we also sent out patrols and set up ambushes to kill the NVA/VC before they attacked us. This day Lieutenant Baxter tasked Mike and me to set up an ambush in front of Second Platoon positions. Two things needed to happen before establishing an ambush site. First, we took a patrol out to find the best ambush site to intercept an enemy force, and, second, we coordinated with Second Platoon to the exact location of the ambush site. We didn't want to receive any friendly fire from the firebase.

In the morning, we formed up the patrol to find the best ambush site. The patrol consisted of Mike, Alabama, Mississippi, Bill Davenport, Rebel (the platoon sergeant's RTO), and me. We departed at 1000 hours, moved through the front gate, and headed east. The patrol moved through an open field and then into thick underbrush and trees. We found an ideal location for the ambush site 500 meters in front of Second Platoon's position. It featured a slight elevation above the surrounding vegetation and had several paths leading toward the firebase. It had good cover and concealment. After marking the grid coordinates of the exact location on the map, we set up a perimeter to eat lunch. We headed back to the firebase after a leisurely lunch.

Once back at the firebase, Mike and I coordinated with Lieutenant Baxter and the Second Platoon Leader on the ambush site location and received their approval. Departure time was 1700 hours and return at 0700 hours. The times were important for Second Platoon to know the patrol's movement. The patrol's RTO communicated with Lieutenant Baxter.

We got in a couple hours of rest before departing. The night would be long. As planned, we departed the front gate at 1700 hours and headed toward the ambush site. This time, we took a different longer route, hoping the enemy didn't realize we were heading back to the same, earlier, location. We arrived at the ambush site at 1815 hours and set up our perimeter, making sure Alabama's M-60 could cover both likely trails. Once comfortable with the fields of fire, we set up trip flares, early warning, and claymore mines to kill the enemy before they got to our positions.

We made sure we maintained a slow pace, used as much conceal-ment as possible, and remained silent. Giving our position away could be fatal. It was getting to be dusk, so we had a cold meal for dinner. I smoked, and I craved a cigarette, but the light and smell of smoke could have given away our position.

As the sun dropped behind the horizon, Bill Davenport told me he had to go potty. Bill was from Washington, my height but heavier, with blond hair, and the biggest smile you ever saw. Bill was always joking and using words such as "potty" for "going to the bathroom" or "din-din" for "dinner." My first reaction was "Hell, no" because he needed to go outside the perimeter. He insisted, so I let him go. Fifteen minutes later, nearly dark, branches of the overgrown vegetation moved to our right front. We tensed up, ready for an NVA patrol to move on us. Then we heard, in English, "Friendly, friendly, friendly coming in." It was Bill returning with his hands in the air as if to surrender. The look on Bill's face as he saw us ready to fire was worth letting him go out. We stifled our laughter to avoid making too much noise. Mike and I looked at each other with huge smiles, acknowledging that it was Bill!

Each hour we called in a sit-rep (situation report) to Lieutenant Baxter, so the command group knew everything was well. We pressed the key on the handset twice (squelch) to send the prearranged negative sit-rep. We didn't talk; the transmission could give away our position to the enemy. The receiving position pressed the handset once to confirm receiving the sit-rep. Enemy soldiers never crossed our path during the long night. The next morning, as the sun came up, we had breakfast and then removed the trip flares and claymore mines. We were thankful that no NVA had come our way. We headed back to Hill 4-11 for a well-deserved rest.

Still working hard on the Hill, we completed more than three weeks of work on FSB Hill 4-11. Work slowed due to rainy weather and lack of materials. Things quieted considerably. The platoon had lost strength, because platoon members got jobs in the rear and we'd had some casualties. Leslie Pressley was assigned as Captain Tyson's RTO and Terry Daron got a job in the rear, so training was needed for the new RTOs. John Meyer became the Lieutenant's RTO, and Rebel became the Platoon Sergeant's RTO. We received one new replacement, James Anderson, from Kentucky, several days before we left the Hill.

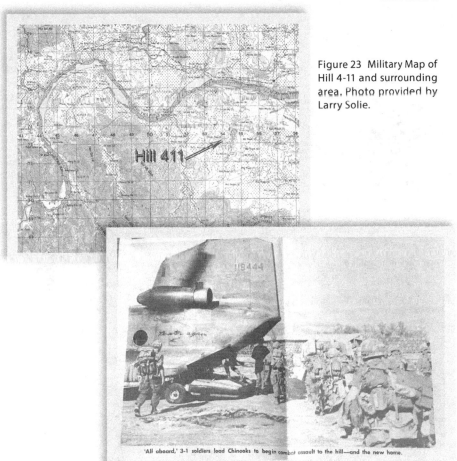

Figure 23 Military Map of Hill 4-11 and surrounding area. Photo provided by Larry Solie.

'All aboard,' 3-1 soldiers load Chinooks to begin combat assault to the hill—and the new home.

Figure 24 First Platoon at FSB Bronco loading on Chinook for transport to Hill 411 July 8, 1969. Photo provided by Charlie Deppen and photo taken by Steve Tippon, *Southern Cross Newspaper*.

Figure 25 First day on Hill 4-11 Captain Tyson with sign dedicating Hill to (KIAs) Sergeant Kelley and Sergeant McCoy. Photo provided by Bob Tyson.

Figure 26 Sergeant Owens with mine sweeper on Hill 4-11 with LT Baxter walking up trail. Photo provided by Charlie Deppen and photo taken by Steve Tippon, *Southern Cross Newspaper.*

Figure 28 Tim "Dusty" Rhoades basic training picture (WIA July 14, 1969). Photo submitted by Dusty Rhoades.

Figure 27 LT Baxter on Hill 4-11. Small bunker to his left is the only shelter against rockets, mortar, sapper attacks and Typhon Tess. Photo provided by Mike Dankert.

Figure 29 Eldon Reynolds (KIA July 14, 1969) Basic Training photo.

Figure 30 Juan Ramos (KIA July 14, 1969) on FSB Cork. Photo provided by Dusty Rhoades.

Figure 31 John Meyer (foreground) and Bill Davenport on stand-down at Chu Lai. Photo provided by Mike Dankert.

Figure 32 FSB Hill 4-11 after March 1970. Note fully constructed bunkers. Photo provided by Louis Bohn.

CHAPTER 6

LEAVING THE HILL

It was early August; the Hill was fortified, and we had completed most of the hard labor. Our defenses needed improvements only here and there, mostly the locations of claymore mines and trip flares in front of our bunkers. Late one afternoon, we were sitting on our bunker, enjoying time for rest and conversation. We noticed to the south of the Hill a line of Vietnamese carrying what appeared to be baskets and other parcel-type items walking west toward the mountains. There were several hundred people in line. The ARVNs told us they were villagers carrying food and supplies to the NVA and VC in the mountains as they prepared for the monsoon season.

Mike looked at the mountains and said, "I don't look forward to climbing them."

I said, "Me, too."

We'd built Firebase Hill 4-11 in 30 days. Now it was our turn to patrol outside the *safety* of the firebase and allow another company to protect the Hill. During the first week of August, the companies patrolling the

AO outside the Hill experienced many confrontations with the enemy and suffered casualties. The enemy shot down several helicopters, wounding or killing crew members. E Troop APCs hit booby traps and suffered casualties, too. It took a short time for us to find a VC presence and a large NVA force waiting for us.

NEW MISSION—AUGUST 7

Our new mission was to patrol around the horseshoe AO located northwest of Hill 4-11 and west of the river. Early that morning the Hueys arrived and transported the platoon to the Horseshoe. We flew in expecting a hot landing zone, so we locked and loaded as we landed. As always, we jumped from the helicopters as fast as possible. Our squad fanned out to give cover for the next two helicopters that came in with the rest of the platoon. The platoon jumped from their helicopters as they landed and moved to thicker vegetation away from the helicopters for cover and concealment. The helicopters took off, heading back to Duc Pho. We joined the rest of the company and patrolled the horseshoe for five days.

On our first day out, we moved through the area toward the river, with no NVA contact. The supply chopper landed as we prepared for evening, and an FNG jumped off and moved to the Command Post (CP) position. Lieutenant Baxter brought the new guy over and introduced him to Jerry Ofstedahl, second squad leader. The new guy was Tommy Thompson from Oklahoma. Jerry introduced Thompson to the rest of the squad. As Jerry introduced Thompson, several of us made eye contact and nodded our head at him. A couple squad members stood and shook his hand. But it was business as usual, and we didn't have time for an FNG.

On the second day, we found what appeared to be an old NVA Prisoner of War (POW) holding camp. We found two old cages made of bamboo large enough to hold two men, rope, and eating utensils. They appeared to have been there a while. One cage held what appeared to be human bones. Lieutenant Baxter called it in, but we never found out if it had held POWs or even if anyone came to investigate.

Later Lanzer came over to talk. Jack Lanzer was from New York and proud of it. Lanzer had arrived at the platoon October 1968, which made him the individual who had been in the platoon the longest. He was always willing to share his stories of life in New York. Lanzer left the unconfirmed impression he had two choices before coming to Vietnam: Going to jail or enlisting in the US Army. We never knew if it was true. He didn't appear the criminal type.

Lanzer was a great storyteller, and his best story was about a bone. He wore a bone around his neck and told every FNG who came into the platoon how he got it, where he got it, and why he wore it. He called it his good luck charm. Lanzer claimed he took it from the body of an NVA soldier he killed. We knew what story Lanzer was telling by the look in the FNG's eyes. Knowing Lanzer, we didn't believe his gruesome story but always pretended we did while talking with him. We were sure it was an animal bone.

He wore a huge Bowie knife that fit in a sheath on his right hip. He claimed that the knife had come to Vietnam with an original platoon member from Hawaii. Lanzer was getting short (tour almost over), so he called me over and said, "Haynie, I have something for you," and handed me the knife. He said the knife was special and passed on to special soldiers. I felt honored to receive the knife and told him I would take care of it and pass it to a special soldier. The next day Lanzer got on the supply chopper and flew back to Duc Pho for a rear job. I passed the Bowie knife on to Bill Davenport in December 1969. Bill was a special soldier, and I hope Lanzer approved.

On the third day a report came from the Battalion Commander, Lieutenant Colonel Ellis, to the Company Commanders and the company Platoon Leaders. There was an intelligence report from the ARVN Division Intelligence (G-2) that, from August 8 to August 15, the VC/NVA troops were expected to infiltrate the district and harass US and ARVN troops.

On the fourth day we stopped by the river to eat lunch. Within minutes the company received small-arms fire from across the river. We hit the ground and took cover. Captain Tyson at once called in artillery on the suspected enemy positions. Seven or eight artillery rounds exploded on target. We received no more incoming rounds from across the river.

On the fifth day Lieutenant Baxter told us of a big, upcoming mission. Lieutenant Colonel Ellis assigned the company to a Battalion Task Force. Right before we left to head to the Hill, we received another replacement for first squad, Gary Morris, from Ohio. Lieutenant Baxter brought the new guy over and introduced him to Joe Mitchell, first squad leader. Joe introduced Morris to the rest of the first squad. Maurice Harrington climbed into the helicopter Morris had arrived on and headed back to Duc Pho to begin his R & R.

We continued to move toward the Hill. There was an occasional sighting of NVA; we received small-arms fire, and we stopped while Captain Tyson called in artillery. We covered four or five klicks and were back at Hill 4-11. We assembled outside the firebase to prepare for our next mission.

PREPARING FOR THE MISSION—AUGUST 12

The company formed up east and south of Hill 4-11 on August 12. After we'd received supplies and ammunition, Lieutenant Baxter briefed us on our mission and told us to expect contact with a large NVA force operating in the AO. Intelligence briefings normally overstated enemy movement and the possibility of contact, so we weren't too concerned.

We were to be part of a Task Force assigned to sweep northwest of Quang Ngai city heading toward the river (Song Tra Bon). The Battalion Commander composed the Task Force of two of the battalion companies, Alpha Company and Bravo Company, with tanks and APCs from E Troop of the First Cavalry, a unit headquartered at Duc Pho. Charlie Company remained west of the Hill, and Delta Company stayed on the Hill for security.

During the day we organized our gear, checked and cleaned our weapons, and ensured we had enough ammunition. We talked of home to pass time. The conversation turned to the usual: Cars, girls, school, and jobs. Being nervous about the upcoming mission, I needed the conversation to take my mind off what the next day might bring. As we sat around taking a break from our preparation of the upcoming mission, I noticed that half the squad were sitting together. I got my camera out and took a photograph of the group (see figure 33).

Figure 33 Preparing for mission August 12, 1969. Seated Left to Right: James Anderson, Danny Carey, Bill Davenport, Ray ("Alabama") Hamilton. Standing: Mike Dankert, Ronald Owens, Jerry Ofstedahl. Photo provided by Glyn Haynie.

Sitting on the ground left to right was James Anderson, Danny Carey, Bill Davenport, and Ray ("Alabama") Hamilton. Standing to the rear of the seated squad members, left to right, was Mike Danker, Ronald Owens and Jerry Ofstedahl. Unknown to us, during the next three days, three squad members in the photograph taken that day would be killed and three wounded.

James Anderson, 20, was from Smith Groves, Kentucky and had a southern drawl. He was one of the newer guys, an FNG, with the squad for only two weeks, having arrived at the platoon the end of July 1969. James married Janice before coming to Vietnam and had no children.

James was quiet but always paid attention to his surroundings, and you could tell he tried to learn as much as possible by watching others. He would get the "F" dropped from the FNG in no time with his positive attitude.

Danny Carey, 20, from Utica, Illinois, was unmarried. Danny liked to kid around and laugh. He found the good in any circumstance. It was great that we had someone with his disposition in the squad. He'd arrived at the platoon the end of June 1969 and was with us when we built the Hill.

Bill Davenport, unmarried, from Longview, Washington, was slightly chubby (for the field). It didn't take him long to prove himself to the squad and platoon. He always had the biggest smile on his face. Bill was fun and always made you smile and laugh. He had a great sense of humor. It took no time for us to develop a friendship. Bill became the assistant machine gunner for Alabama and performed his job well.

Alabama—Ray Hamilton—was from a small town in Alabama, hence his nickname, and he, too, had a Southern drawl. He had arrived at the platoon in early June 1969 with many other replacements. Alabama married Donne before coming to Vietnam and had no children. He was quiet but always engaged in conversation and a welcome addition to the squad. He had an easy, small grin; when he talked, you were comfortable with him. Being religious, Alabama read his bible every day. Devoted to his wife, he wrote her most days. He became an excellent M-60 machine gunner; he could always be counted on to protect the squad.

Mike Dankert had arrived in Vietnam March 1969 but didn't get to the platoon until early May 1969. He was on emergency leave home during the month of April. Mike and I hit it off at once, and our relationship developed into a friendship. He accepted responsibility without question and was developing into a leader. Mike mentored and watched over the newer guys. I think most of the squad looked up to Mike. He was serious but could loosen up, given the opportunity. Man, was he stubborn!

Ronald Owens was serving in the National Guard as a sergeant and had worked for the US Postal Service before being called to active duty.

He was from Wichita, Kansas, and had arrived at the platoon early June 1969. He wasn't too tall, but chubby, with dark hair. I'm unsure of his age, but he was older than most of us. He stayed with the command group most of the time and occasionally served as a team leader in the squad. Ronald liked to talk and did so on many topics. We found most of his conversations entertaining.

Jerry Ofstedahl, from Napa, California, was the squad leader for second squad. Jerry had arrived at the platoon December 1968, which made him an old-timer with experience. He'd married Claire, his longtime girlfriend, while on R & R to Tokyo, Japan, the month before; he had no children. I found Jerry to be an outstanding leader and fair, someone I wanted to emulate. He always shared his experiences and knowledge to help us survive our year in Vietnam.

The squad members not in the picture that day were Frank Brown, Charlie Deppen, Tommy Thompson, Donald Cameron, and me.

Frank Brown, 19, was a large man at six feet tall, maybe taller, and easily 175 pounds. He was from Grand Rapids, Michigan and had arrived at the platoon in late June 1969. Frank carried the M-79 grenade launcher and became proficient at firing on a target and fast at re-loading. He was dependable and quiet but friendly to the members of the squad. The squad members liked and trusted Frank.

Charlie Deppen, 21, was from Tampa, Florida. Charlie was quiet and kept to himself. It appeared he was reluctant to get to know the squad members or let them know him. He associated with the other new guys who'd arrived with him in early June, especially Alabama. He'd looked up to Tufts, and his death affected him. Bridge was his favorite topic, which we found odd, thinking it more of an old person's card game.

Tommy Thompson, 21, was the newest member, an FNG, of the second squad, joining us around August 8, 1969. He was from Bristow, Oklahoma. Tommy married Connie before coming to Vietnam and had no children. He arrived after we'd built the Hill. The squad talked about the Hill often, and I'm sure Tommy felt left out of the conversation. I didn't know Tommy well, but he came across as likeable and ready to learn.

Donald Cameron was from California. I'm not sure of his arrival date—maybe in June 1969. He had his college degree and was older than most of us at 22 years old. Don had an interest in law enforcement or had worked in law enforcement before being drafted into the Army. It may be he wanted to be a lawyer. Don was not shy voicing his opinion, whether he'd been asked for it or not. Don and I had a strange relationship. We got along OK. I don't think he liked me much, but I believe I had his respect.

I'd grown an inch in the last six months but had lost more weight. I was considered a veteran in the platoon and was more confident in my abilities walking point and mentoring the newer guys. I'm sure my baby-face, at first, led the FNGs to believe that I was too young to help them, but as time went by, I earned their trust. Mike's and my friendship turned into being brothers. One couldn't be found without the other. He even put up with several of my immature moments.

Looking in the opposite direction of my squad, I saw first squad preparing for the mission and many having conversations, like second squad. I knew most of first squad. Being in the squad several months ago, I still felt a friendship with them. As I looked around, I spotted the squad members I knew: Joe Mitchell, John DeLoach, Ryan Okino, Barry Suda, Paul Ponce, Chuck Council, and Garry Morris. Maurice Harrington had left a couple days previous to go on R & R, so he was not there.

Joe Mitchell, first squad leader, was from Chicago, Illinois. Joe had arrived at the platoon November 1968, which made him an old-timer with experience. He and his wife, Barbara, had no children. Joe was always friendly, talkative, and willing to share his experiences and knowledge with the squad members. We were never close, but he taught me a lot.

Mississippi—John DeLoach—was from Mississippi, hence his nickname. He, too, had a Southern drawl. Mississippi was a big man, standing six feet, two inches. I at once liked John, and we became friends. I am sure we looked like Mutt and Jeff standing next to each other. He took my place as the youngest platoon member upon his arrival to the platoon in early June 1969. He talked about his father's ranch, and riding horses was his passion. He had an easygoing personality; nothing appeared to upset him.

Ryan Okino, 19, was serving in the National Guard and came to Vietnam on a six-month tour. He was from Hilo, Hawaii. He stood five feet, six inches tall and had dark hair—finally someone shorter than me! Ryan liked to joke around; he was friendly and quick to join in a conversation. He'd arrived at the platoon in early June 1969. He was at the bunker the night the enemy killed Ramos and Reynolds, and he helped Dusty. You could see more sadness in his eyes, and he appeared quieter since that day. He impressed me with how he carried and handled the M-60 for the squad, even with his small stature.

Barry Suda, from Honolulu, Hawaii, was also a National Guardsman on a six-month tour. He was friendly but quiet, always appearing serious. Barry had arrived at the platoon in early June 1969. Barry talked little, but you could tell he was always paying attention. Everyone liked Barry; he was a good soldier and an asset to the platoon—someone you could count on during tough times.

Paul Ponce, from Santa Clara, California, had arrived at the platoon in November 1968. He and his wife, Juanita, had no children. I learned years later that Paul had a son conceived while on R & R. Paul was always friendly and talkative, and he would give you the shirt off his back if you needed it. He'd gone to Hawaii on R & R to meet his wife and was happy upon his return to the squad. As I looked at Paul, I reached up, held my peace sign, and gave it a rub for him.

Chuck Council was from Portland, Oregon. At 23, he was older than most of us—hence his nickname, "Pops." He'd arrived at the platoon in April 1969. Even though we were never in the same squad, Chuck and I became friends. Chuck was older and had gone to college. I looked up to Chuck because he listened to you and gave good advice. He was outspoken about the war, staying pissed at America, the Army, and anyone else who had something to do with us going to war. I can't blame him. With that said, he always smiled, and his eyes had a twinkle of happiness when he was around the platoon. He carried the M-79 for first squad.

Garry Morris was the newest member, an FNG, of the first squad and platoon, joining around August 11, 1969. I didn't know Gary. He came across as likeable and appeared to be fitting in with first squad. He was from Lancaster, Ohio.

Maurice Harrington was from North Carolina. He'd arrived at the platoon November 1968, which made him an old-timer. Maurice was always quick with a smile and a joke. I found him entertaining and friendly. He was a great distraction to our surroundings. On the serious side, he could take charge and be a team leader or squad leader. He didn't know it at the time, but he was lucky that he chose this week to go on R & R.

Then I moved my gaze over to the center and noticed the platoon command group preparing for the mission, too. The platoon leader, Lieutenant Baxter, and platoon sergeant, Staff Sergeant Swindle, were studying a map together. The two RTOs, John Meyer and Rebel, were changing out the batteries on their radios.

Lieutenant John Baxter, from Gainesville, Florida, had a college degree and had been in the Peace Corps before entering the Army. Lieutenant Baxter arrived in Vietnam in March 1969 and at the platoon in early April 1969; he was assigned as the first platoon leader. Lieutenant Baxter was aloof personally but approachable by the platoon members, and he listened to what you had to say. He proved to be an effective and outstanding leader. He had the respect and trust of the platoon. We would follow him anywhere.

Staff Sergeant Robert Swindle was from Fort Lauderdale, Florida. He was married to Celsa and had a son. Staff Sergeant Swindle, a career soldier, had arrived at the platoon in June 1969 and was assigned as the platoon sergeant. His assignment to Vietnam was in February 1969, but I'm not sure what his first job was. I didn't know him personally but respected him as our platoon sergeant. He, too, was aloof. He maintained a professional relationship and didn't socialize with the members of the platoon.

Rebel, Richard Wellman, from Gastonia, North Carolina, also had a Southern drawl. That's how he got the nickname Rebel. He was 20 and had married his wife, Deborah, before coming to Vietnam. He'd received his assignment to the platoon March 1969. Rebel was quiet but always willing to speak if you engaged him in conversation. He proved himself during his first six months while in the first squad and was assigned as the platoon sergeant RTO after Terry Daron left for a rear job.

John Meyer, 20, was from Wisconsin. John had received his assignment to the platoon in October 1968. He was talkative and liked to joke. John got care packages from home, and they always contained his favorite item, Coors beer! John loved music and knew the current artists and songs. He tried to sing along, but I don't think he sang that well. He proved himself during his first six months while in the second squad and was assigned as the platoon leader RTO after Leslie Pressley left for a rear job. John led a charmed life; he never got a scratch.

We put our equipment away and made dinner. I had my usual beef with spice sauce, peanut butter and cracker crunch, pears, pound cake, and hot chocolate. I removed a Coke from my rucksack to enjoy later on guard duty and dug a shallow hole to set the Coke in so it would be cool during the early morning of my guard shift. As the sun was disappearing, I lit my last cigarette of the day. Mike and I talked of the mission and thought we would do well with the large size of the task force. Once I'd finished my cigarette, we called it a night, rolled up in our poncho liners, and went to sleep, surrounded by tanks and APCs.

AMBUSH—AUGUST 13

The Task Force was impressive, with tanks and APCs from E Troop 1/1 Cav, and two infantry companies, Alpha and Bravo of our battalion. Staff Sergeant Swindle instructed us to travel light, so we placed our rucksacks on a specific APC designated for our platoon. For this mission, we carried only our weapons, ammo, grenades, water, one meal, and first aid bandages. Captain Tyson assigned First Platoon as the point platoon for the Task Force's right-flank security. Lieutenant Baxter had second squad take the point position within the platoon. Jerry told me to take point.

As we moved out at 0700 hours, Lieutenant Baxter told me to head in an easterly direction toward the river. We moved through rice paddies and meadows with vegetation around us. The metallic sounds of the APCs rattling as we traversed the AO was strange because, working and moving as a platoon, we always tried to keep dead silence. I heard the crack of gunfire, and then gunships flew over us to fire on an enemy position. I thought other platoons or companies had contacted the NVA.

Bravo Company was the unit in the center of the Task Force and in front of most of the APCs and tanks. Alpha Company was on both sides of the APC column as it moved east, and First Platoon was on the right flank with several APCs between the two squads. Second squad was the furthest out to the right flank.

I walked point, and Mike walked drag, the last man in the formation. Staff Sergeant Swindle and his RTO, Rebel, squad leader Jerry Ofstedahl, our machine gunner Alabama, assistant gunner Bill Davenport, Don Cameron, Danny Carey, Frank Brown, Charles Deppen, Tommy Thompson, and James Anderson were between Mike and me. Our side of the column moved in a staggered column formation with ten feet between each squad member, and me leading the way.

At 1200 hours we moved through thick vegetation alternating with open areas. To my right was a thick stand of small trees, bamboo, and vegetation. A trench more than seven feet deep and eight feet wide ran parallel between our path and the tree line. Walking 20 meters in front of Cameron and the rest of the squad, I approached an opening on the right and across the trench, 30 meters away. I spotted what appeared to be a bunker. I told Cameron that a bunker was ahead, that I'd check it out, and that the platoon should stop moving forward.

I moved past the hedgerow and into the opening. I ran down the trench and up the opposite side. As I reached the top of the trench, I stopped one foot out. I saw a head sticking up from the top of the bunker; he spotted me at the same time. I at once identified the individual as NVA by his uniform.

I don't know why, but I shouted, "Lai dai, mother fucker," which means "Come here now."

I shouted back to Cameron, "Gooks are ahead—move the platoon back."

The soldier disappeared; he ran out of the bunker and across an open field away from me. I took up a kneeling firing position and fired several three-round bursts at the running soldier. He fell, but he got back up and stumbled into the tree line. I fired several more rounds but lost him in the thick vegetation.

As I watched the soldier stumble into the tree line, all hell broke loose. Automatic weapons were firing, and there were explosions at the squad position to my right rear 30 meters away. I could tell by the sound that M-16 and AK-47 weapons were firing, too. I waited; I couldn't see through the thick hedgerow that separated me from the squad. Within minutes, two NVA soldiers burst through the tree line 20 meters to my right front. They were moving away from where the weapons were firing. I at once leveled my M-16 as the NVA on the left and I made eye contact and fired off three to four rounds, hitting him in the chest and head. He took several steps backward and fell to the ground. This startled the second soldier, and he stopped running. I don't think he expected me to be there. He appeared confused or maybe scared. Hell—me, too. I pointed my weapon and squeezed off a fast burst of three to six rounds, hitting him in the chest. He fell to the ground next to his comrade.

I needed to reload, so I pushed the button to release the used magazine, dropping it to the ground. Reaching into my bandoleer tied around my waist, I removed a new magazine. I inserted the new magazine, pulled the charging handle back, and released it to load a bullet into the chamber.

Bullets zinged by my head and body, and dirt kicked up to my left side; the firing was coming from my rear. My first thought was that Cameron had opened fire behind me. I turned and yelled, "Cameron, quit fucking firing!" But I didn't see Cameron on the other side of the trench. I looked downward and saw an NVA soldier in a spider hole in the trench 30 feet from me. His head and AK-47 protruded from the hole. His eyes looked huge, and his face was wet with sweat; he looked at me in disbelief that I was still standing. Many thoughts raced through my mind. Primarily, I was "behind the lines," and I needed to get to the squad across the trench. My heart was pounding so fast and hard that I could hear it beating. I slid downward along the trench, using the heel of my right boot to slow my descent while firing a full magazine at the enemy soldier. I watched chunks of his skull fly into the trench wall behind him as his pith helmet rolled downward to the bottom of the trench. I didn't stop until I knew he wasn't firing or moving.

I don't know why, because most of my 20 bullets had hit him in the face and head, but I stopped to check the enemy soldier to make sure I'd killed him. After checking the soldier, I released the empty magazine from my M-16 and let it hit the ground. I inserted a new magazine and loaded a bullet into the chamber. Scared, I looked to my left and right for more enemy soldiers. I could hardly breathe because of the fear taking hold of my body. I had to get out of the trench and back to the squad. Not seeing any enemy and gasping for air, I crawled upward, out of the trench, to our side and the squad.

As I got closer to the squad position, the APCs, in reverse, moved away from the squad while the enemy fired automatic weapons and RPGs (Rocket-Propelled Grenades). Mississippi lay in a prone position 30 meters away from me, not far from the APC positions, in the grass, facing the enemy. I watched in horror as an APC moving in reverse drove right over him. I thought for sure the track had killed him, but as soon as the APC had cleared his position, Mississippi sat up. What a relief! RPGs and machine-gun fire had hit several APCs. The Cav wounded and dead were lying next to a berm surrounded by APCs. One of the APCs was on fire.

My memory about the situation at that point is vague. My adrenaline was pumping to the maximum from the fear, physical exertion, facing the enemy, and the unknown. I concentrated on the enemy and what I had to do, so I was not aware what everyone around me was doing, nor do I recall the exact sequence of events.

As I ran to the tree line and squad position, I came upon Cameron first and three bodies lying a few feet from the trench. Cameron was in a hedgerow with thick trees for cover and brush for concealment. Cameron was facing the direction I'd come from and turned to watch me moving back to the squad position.

I stopped and asked Cameron, "Did you check them?"

Cameron said, "No."

I gave Cameron a disapproving stare and shouted, "Cover me" at Alabama and Davenport, concealed behind a small berm 20 feet from my position. Alabama fired his M-60, with Davenport feeding the belts of ammo for him. The bullets cut through the dense tree line across the trench to our front.

I crawled to where the bodies had fallen and checked Rebel first, and then Swindle, and Jerry last. Thinking I heard Jerry moan, I rolled him over into my arms.

Yelling at Cameron, I said, "Jerry is alive!"

Don shook his head and said, "No." He must have already known.

I looked at Jerry, and I, too, knew he was dead. I noticed Jerry lying on two grenades that must have fallen off Rebel as he hit the ground. For some unknown reason, I picked them up and put them in my side shirt pocket. The three were dead. The enemy soldiers were still firing at us and the squad continued to fire back.

I crawled back to our position and moved along the line of squad members to check on them and to find Mike. I saw Frank Brown lying on his back and crawled to his body, lying not far from the others, and checked for signs of life. Frank was alive—but barely. The enemy had shot him in the head and right leg, and he was in shock. I sat Frank up, cradling his head against my chest, and noticed him biting down hard; he had blood running from his nose. I tried to open his mouth so he wouldn't bite his tongue. My only thought was to open his mouth so he could breathe. I panicked, feeling overwhelmed with Frank's wounds and blood, and I didn't know what to do. Needing help, I called for a medic. Mike ran over; then a medic showed up, and they both worked on Brown. We were still receiving fire from the enemy; there were explosions, and bullets were flying everywhere. I fired back into the dense vegetation, not seeing any enemy.

Several tracks moved to our position, and we used their cover to move Brown back to a safe location behind the tracks. While Mike and the medic continued to work on Brown, a dust-off landed and picked up E Troop's two wounded and two killed. Once loaded with the wounded, the helicopter took flight. A second dust-off arrived, and Mike, with two other guys and me, loaded Frank onto the chopper. Frank was a heavy man. The Huey took off, heading to the Division Hospital at Chu Lai. During this time, the squad provided covering fire for the dust-off helicopters.

I went over to Mike after the dust-off carrying Frank had taken flight, and Mike asked, "What happened?"

"There are gooks everywhere, and I fired on them," I replied. Mike then knew that those first shots he'd heard were from me.

I said, "I told Cameron to have the squad move back."

"We didn't receive the word," Mike replied. The firefight may have happened so fast that Cameron didn't have time to pass it.

We saw Swindle, Jerry, and Rebel lying where they had fallen. Mike noticed the radio lying with Rebel.

Mike said, "We need the radio."

I thought, *Shit—I didn't get the radio!*

We looked at each other.

Mike said, "I'll get it."

Mike yelled to Alabama, "Cover me."

Alabama and the rest of us opened fire to cover Mike as he crawled out to the radio. Mike had to move Rebel so he could retrieve the radio. He crawled back with the radio as we continued to give covering fire. Once Mike was back to a safe position, he radioed Lieutenant Baxter and told him of our location and those killed and wounded.

We knew we couldn't get Jerry, Swindle, and Rebel out unless we had more firepower. I noticed one APC, without gunners, sitting not too far away. The driver and the .50 caliber gunner were alone on it. Mike and I ran to the APC, climbed on, and took over the two mounted M-60 machine guns, one on each side of the APC—Mike on the left gun and me on the right gun. I instructed the driver to move forward so we could give covering fire, allowing us to get to Jerry, Swindle, and Rebel.

The driver didn't want to move; I explained to him we needed the APC to give covering fire to get our dead and wounded out. This convinced him to help us. As the APC moved forward, we heard a loud thud to the front right of the APC, and the APC stopped.

I asked, "What happened? Why are we were stopping?"

The gunner said, "An RPG hit us, but it was a dud."

I yelled to the driver, "Keep moving forward!"

The APC reached the fallen platoon members and moved into position not far from where they lay. We assisted in providing covering fire with the mounted M-60 machine guns. As the .50 caliber gunner fired, the trees fell over as if an invisible giant was cutting them.

Mike and I dismounted the APC to check on the squad and to help retrieve the three dead. I know we got Jerry, Rebel, and Staff Sergeant Swindle but I don't remember recovering them or who helped. As soon as Mike and I got off the APC, the driver threw it into reverse and moved back to the other APCs. I don't remember seeing NVA—just shooting back at bullets coming toward us. The enemy was still firing a .51 caliber machine gun, small arms, and RPGs at the platoon.

I moved back to Lieutenant Baxter and first squad's location, while Mike took charge of the squad to make sure they deployed with the least exposure to enemy weapons fire. The first squad was in a line, lying against a C-shaped berm, with Lieutenant Baxter on one end and Chuck Council at the other. I moved next to Lieutenant Baxter and briefed him on what had happened and those killed and wounded. While talking, I looked downward at my shaking hands and noticed two lit cigarettes between my fingers. After I'd briefed Lieutenant Baxter, I looked toward Chuck Council. I saw the questioning look Chuck had in his eyes. I shook my head side to side and moved back to the second squad position.

Lieutenant Baxter formed up the platoon with support from the APCs engaging the enemy. There were several assaults, led by Lieutenant Baxter, from 1330 hours to past sundown. We still received small-arms, machine-gun, and RPG fire from the other side of the trench. We had artillery support, but it didn't deter the enemy. Later someone called in gunships to fire their mini-guns and rockets to destroy the enemy positions and make the enemy retreat. During this time a dust-off landed, and we loaded Jerry, Swindle, and Rebel. Once loaded, the dust-off took flight to Duc Pho. We used plenty of firepower against the enemy, but they were relentless and didn't retreat. They were only several hundred feet from us and had excellent cover and concealment. They were dug in!

We received instructions to move back and to move quickly because Shadow was coming to cover us as we moved away from the enemy and to protect our perimeter. Captain Tyson called in flare ships to illuminate the battlefield. We were losing daylight, and we noticed that the APCs had left, heading back to the Hill. The APC with our rucksacks had dumped them in a pile as they left. We spent most of the evening trying to maneuver to the rucksacks, as they contained our resupply of ammo, water, and food.

We moved through the tall grass with only the moonlight and the illumination of the flares to guide us toward the rucksacks. At one point, as I followed the person in front of me, I sensed someone standing off the trail to my right, and I leveled my M-16, determining in time that it was a woman with a female child about six years old. She looked terrified, and I thought it strange that she and the child were standing there in the middle of this firefight. I wished they had passed it back that someone was on the trail. I passed their location to the person behind me.

We reached the pile of rucksacks and had to low crawl out to get one—it didn't matter whose—and move back to the platoon. It took 30 minutes to retrieve the rucksacks. We had to get the four rucksacks that belonged to Jerry, Swindle, Rebel, and Brown, too. During the time we were retrieving the rucksacks, we could hear and see overhead the mini-gun ships firing at the enemy.

We arrived at our night position exhausted, scared, thirsty, and hungry. We set up our defenses and fields of fire and guard shifts, but it was too late to set out claymores and trip flares. As we lay there in silence, I found and opened a can of chicken noodles, ate it cold, and washed the meal down with warm water. I wanted a cigarette but dared not light one. Mike and I lay next to each other and stayed awake, waiting for the NVA. Fortunately, they didn't come.

DESTROY THE TUNNELS—AUGUST 14

As the sun appeared on the horizon, we felt relief. We gathered around a berm, exchanging rucksacks to claim our own and fix breakfast. Someone told Mississippi not to move. An unexploded RPG round was sticking out of the rucksack he'd retrieved the previous night. Everyone unconsciously took a step backward, away from Mississippi. He sat still, waiting for help. Sweat beaded his face and dripped to the ground. Someone approached him and removed the round; it was a dud, and we discarded it. Mississippi had a charmed two days!

While I was heating my hot chocolate, Lieutenant Baxter came over and asked, "Did anyone deserve an award for yesterday?"

I said, "Yes, Dankert took charge of the squad, killed enemy soldiers, helped repel the enemy attack, and, while still receiving fire, helped save Frank Brown's life. He went out under fire to retrieve the radio to contact you, and, later, while still under fire, he helped get Jerry, Swindle, and Rebel."

Lieutenant Baxter said, "Roger that," and walked away.

After breakfast I went over to one of the "extra" rucksacks and retrieved two bandoleers of M-16 ammunition. The rucksack belonged to Rebel. I'd used 10 to 15 of mine and didn't recover most of the empty magazines during the firefight, leaving them where they fell.

In the morning hours after breakfast, Mike and I took a patrol out to search the surrounding area for any enemy. We had been right to hurry to the previous night's logger. As we walked, we saw more than 10 dead NVA killed the night before and how the mini-guns and artillery had torn the earth up where the fighting had taken place. A search of their pockets and gear yielded letters and maps, possible intelligence. Returning to the platoon position, we turned the materials over to Lieutenant Baxter. I don't know who took the body count because we kept on moving. It was later reported that one document recovered, from one NVA company commander to another, stated that there were three NVA companies at the location where the battle had begun on the 13th.

Lieutenant Baxter received orders to find and destroy tunnels. The platoon moved out in an easterly direction toward the river with me on point. We moved through a seemingly deserted village, but I sensed the NVA presence. Lieutenant Baxter had us hold up a klick outside the village. We set up security for a landing zone for the supply helicopter. After 20 minutes, we got word of the supply helicopter approaching, so we popped smoke to signal the landing location for the pilot. The supply helicopter landed and dropped off a dog team and several cases of concussion grenades and fragmentation grenades for the platoon. We placed the four rucksacks and weapons (belonging to Jerry, Swindle, Rebel, and Brown) on the supply helicopter with instructions to take them to the company headquarters. Once unloaded and the rucksacks and weapons placed on board, the supply helicopter lifted off and took flight back to the Hill. Mike and I loaded up with concussion grenades.

We often heard "Fire in the hole" and an explosion. We blew more than 25 tunnels that day. Sometimes a soldier had to enter a tunnel to discover weapons, food, supplies, and/or enemy soldiers. Being a small person, I was the perfect size to be a Tunnel Rat. During my time with the platoon, I'd descended into several tunnels. This mission I disliked most. After removing my gear, I climbed into the tunnel with only a pistol and knife. I often found many signs of life, including lanterns, prepared meals, reading material, and sleeping mats. One of the main goals of a Tunnel Rat was to find a cache of weapons and ammunition. I was very fortunate that I never encountered enemy soldiers!

On this occasion, dog teams with handlers went with us to sniff out the tunnels. I was happy, thinking that, after the dog found the hole, the handler sent the dog into the tunnel. It didn't work that way.

I said to the handler, "Here's an entrance. Send in the dog" as I found a tunnel entrance.

"My dog only finds tunnels and does not go into the tunnel; that job is for the Tunnel Rat," replied the handler.

I said, "Hell, we can find the tunnels. Send in the dog!" I then dropped a concussion grenade into the tunnel opening and yelled, "Fire in the hole." Fuck the dog handler and dog! Within two hours, the dog got hot and tired, so the handler and dog left the field.

On this specific day, we had blown many tunnels as we moved through the AO. Mike and I came upon what appeared to be a cave entrance not far from the riverbank.

I said, "Let's throw our grenades, move on, and find the next one."

Mike sat at the cave entrance and said, "We can't blow this one."

I asked, "Why?"

He said, "It could be used for ammo storage."

"Mike, the tunnels we've blown so far could've been used for ammo storage," I replied.

Mike continued to sit there and said, "We can't blow this one."

I said, "OK" and sat with him. He could be so stubborn!

The platoon found a defensible location and stopped. Exhausted and needing rest, we set up our positions and had our evening meal. The platoon was in a circle of tanks and APCs. Damn, I felt safe. Every so often, a tank started its engine and let it idle. The noise they created wasn't comforting, and we were afraid of giving the enemy our exact location. We requested that they not start the tanks, but they told us the tanks had to be started every so often. I didn't sleep well.

This is a letter from Charlie Deppen to his mother and father dated August 14, 1969.

Dear Mom and Dad,

We've been out in the Quang Ngai valley for the past week. Things were only slightly hectic until yesterday when we linked up with some tanks and APCs to sweep a section of the valley. A little before noon we made contact and we fought till dark. Don't worry about me; I'm perfectly ok. However; we put our rucksacks on the APCs and mine was either lost or more probably blown to pieces by enemy grenades. I lost all my books, my letters (maybe by enemy hands so watch the mail for enemy propaganda), my gear, and my bridge booklets and addresses. My checkbook and wallet are also gone. All my ID cards, etc . . . will have to be replaced as will my glasses. What a mess, Please send me a small address book.

Write soon and keep your fingers crossed for me and my buddies.

Love Charlie

COMMAND DETONATED BOMB—AUGUST 15

We woke to the fumes of diesel and tank engines still running. We started breakfast; we were quiet because of the last few days' events. The platoon didn't have a Platoon Sergeant or a Squad Leader to give us guidance. Mike and I tried to pick up the role of squad leader and got the squad organized for the day's mission. The squad continued to be right-flank security for the task force and point squad for the platoon and company. The mission was to find and destroy the NVA battalion that had been attacking us.

I took point for the platoon, and Mike took up the drag position for the squad. Behind me and to the right was second squad: Anderson, Thompson, Alabama, Davenport, Danny Carey, Deppen, Cameron, and then Mike. To my left rear was first squad: Ponce, Mitchell, the first squad leader, Okino, Suda, Council, Mississippi, and Morris. Lieutenant Baxter, John Meyer (RTO), and Ronald Owens were between both squads, in the middle and way back. First squad had a tank and several APCS to their left.

We moved back through the deserted village and proceeded toward the river. I wondered why the villagers had left. We stopped for lunch at this point. Although not hungry, I ate fruit and crackers with cheese, and drank a whole quart of Kool-Aid. The squad was still quiet and alert to the surroundings. At 1330 hours, we got the order to move out. Lieutenant Baxter told me to head west, away from the river, and then we cut back in a northerly direction.

Around 1600 hours, I moved in a north-by-northeast direction across rice paddies toward the river; behind me, the platoon walked in a staggered column formation with 10 to 15 feet between each person. I moved from one paddy to another, always searching for booby traps and any sign of enemy positions. As we moved forward, I had a hedgerow to my left, a small hedgerow to my right rear, and a large hedgerow to the front 100 meters away. There was nothing but a vacant field between it and me.

Halfway into the field, I slowed my pace; my gut tightened, and the hair stood up on the back of my neck. Every nerve in my body screamed "Danger!" I sensed enemy eyes watching us, and I am sure I smelled the NVA.

I turned and shouted, "Spread out!" and motioned to the platoon to spread out as I shouted the command.

Turning back to face the front, a shock wave of brutal force slammed into me. The force blew me backwards 30 feet through the air as my weapon and gear were ripped away from me. While I was in the air, the sky turned into black smoke and dirt, and then I hit the ground, hard. A 250-pound command-detonated bomb had exploded.

The next thing I knew I was sitting in a tunnel overlooking the battlefield. The air was cool, and the light was dim; muffled voices were speaking at the other end of the tunnel, though none of the voices sounded familiar. Sitting there, I thought how peaceful, cool, and comfortable I was and that I would stay here and not return.

Looking downwards, I saw my platoon members and heard their moans and groans of pain and someone crying for his mother; there were mangled bodies lying everywhere. I saw Ronald Owens turning my body over, searching for wounds. Mike called "Glyn!" I gasped for air as Ronald Owens applied chest compressions. I was on the ground, confused as to what had happened. Owens had saved my life—or was it Mike?

Owens helped me off the field and placed me in an APC with other wounded platoon members. Deppen sat with a blank stare and a large piece of shrapnel sticking out of his right knee. Okino lay on a stretcher, covered in blood and his legs mangled. He was moaning and in shock. Thompson, between cries of pain from the large opening blown in his side, looked around the track in shock, too. Blood-soaked bandages, pools of blood, and chunks of flesh covered the floor. I thought I would be sick, so I moved out of the APC and stumbled to the small berm next to the hedgerow.

I sat on the ground and cried. As I sobbed like a child, Lieutenant Baxter came over and spoke in a calming voice, telling me the platoon needed me. His reassuring voice and words helped me pull myself somewhat together.

I noticed a member of first squad still in the rice paddy. It was Paul Ponce, lying face down and not moving. I got Chuck Council, or Chuck got me, and we moved out to help him. We rolled him over, and I knew that Paul was dead. I saw the huge pool of blood under his body. Tears rolled down my cheeks.

I didn't have a weapon, so I picked up Paul's M-16 that had been lying under his body and used the sling to hold the weapon across my shoulder to get my hands free. Chuck stood there staring at Paul. I nudged him and told him we had to move. We picked up Paul's body, with me picking up his legs from the back of the knee and Chuck reaching under his arms. We lifted and carried him back to the APC. As we carried Paul, I watched blood drip from his wounds and leave a trail behind us. We laid Paul next to Anderson and Carey and covered him with a poncho. I left Chuck with Paul.

I then moved along the hedgerow to another wounded soldier, and, as I approached, there were two soldiers putting the wounded soldier on a stretcher. They each grabbed the handles at opposite ends of the stretcher and lifted the wounded soldier and walked toward me. As they walked by me, I saw the wounded soldier, Joe Mitchell.

I walked alongside the stretcher, talking to Joe as he stared up at me with wide-open eyes and a smile, hoping to comfort him. As we moved, Joe's M-16, which had been lying across his chest, fell off and landed on the ground. The two stretcher-bearers stopped, and I reached to the ground, picked up his M-16, and placed it back on his chest. We started walking again, and I took hold of his hand as if to comfort Joe. I soon realized he wasn't looking at me, listening to my words, or smiling at me. He was dead. My eyes welled up with tears. They moved Joe back to the APC and laid him next to Paul Ponce. The soldiers who had carried Joe covered him with a poncho.

As Mike and I leaned against the APC, we passed a canteen back and forth, not saying a word. Chuck stood next to us with a vacant stare. To our front lay four bodies, each covered by a poncho. We were waiting for the dust-off to get the wounded; I saw Chuck dart toward the four bodies and pull the poncho off Paul, his best friend. Chuck fell to his knees and cried. Mike and I went to Chuck, pulled the poncho back over Paul, and led Chuck away.

We heard the dust-off approaching the landing zone and provided covering fire as the Huey landed. We loaded Charlie Deppen, Ryan Okino, and Tommy Thompson onto the dust-off first. Lieutenant Baxter had platoon members put Alabama and Bill Davenport on the dust-off, and I helped Mike onto the dust-off. Lieutenant Baxter told me to get on, and I told him I would stay until we got replacements. After we loaded the wounded, the pilot took flight. Dust-off pilots are the bravest of the brave. As the helicopter flew away, I looked around and noticed that there were 11 platoon members left out of the 28 we'd started with in July. Platoon members wounded who later returned to the platoon were Mike Dankert, Alabama, and Bill Davenport.

Minutes later, the last dust-off landed to take the dead. After loading them into the waiting dust-off, we stood there and watched Joe

Mitchell, Paul Ponce, James Anderson, and Danny Carey leave for the last time.

Don Cameron came over and said, "Haynie, thank you for staying."

I replied, "Thanks. We need to stay together and protect the squad and platoon the best we can." Cameron's statement surprised me because I didn't think he liked me much.

Chuck Council wrote this letter to a lifelong friend years later.

Dear Jill,

Quang Ngai Valley, August 1969—

As I observe the scene unfolding before me, as far as I can see in every direction, I see the troops and the materiel of war: tanks, solders, artillery of war, armored vehicles of all kinds. This is a search and destroy operation—to search out the enemy and destroy him and destroy his home and destroy his sustenance—to kill. I am here to kill. A song begins to run through my mind, "The Eve of Destruction" by Barry McGuire. And I realize that we are the Eve of Destruction. Indeed, the Eve of Destruction is Me!

A Fire Fight—

Contact with the Enemy. A life and death struggle. And the carnage begins. Soon, all too soon, the cry goes out: MEDIC! MEDIC! All around me the ground is littered with the dead and dying. Brave young men cry for their mothers. Why do some die so arbitrarily while others live so arbitrarily? I have not a scratch on me.

As the contact commences, initially there is a rushing sensation, a kind of high with intensity quite unlike anything else in the human experience. There is no drug one can take to duplicate this high. Some men devote their entire lives to military command just to experience those few fleeting moments when you hold in your hand the power of life and death over another human being. And some men go into a blackout, a blind rage which devastates them and from which they never recover.

But the high is only fleeting. Very quickly it is replaced with a numbing fear and excruciating terror. I once heard it said that when there are no more decisions to be made the fear goes away. That may be true enough but what you're left with is an indescribable horrible feeling of loneliness and emptiness. There is no place to go, no place to hide, no place to get away from it. "—come and get me you little bastards, come and get me—." In a sense your soul has abandoned your body in anticipation of death and in that sense one is truly alone.

Suddenly—

An enormous explosion a short distance off to my right flank. Dust, debris, and black smoke shoot high into the air. Oh, dear, God. Who will die today? I run over to see what's happened. I find our platoon lieutenant and a couple of others crouched down behind a rice paddy dike. The lieutenant says one of our guys is lying out in the rice paddy 10 or 12 yards in front of us. I peer over the top of the dike. I see someone out there lying face down in the dirt. Is he dead, is he alive, we can't even tell who it is. We have to go out and get him. As the others put down a cover of rifle fire I jump over the top of the dike and run out into the rice paddy. I reach down, grab him by the shoulder and roll him over. I'm momentarily stunned. It's my friend, Ponce, my closest friend. He is lying in a pool DEAD! Just moments before on a short rest break we had talked and laughed together. And exchanged cynical jokes about the absurdity of it all. I recoiled back like having hot venom splashed in my eyes. For an instant time stands still: and the image of death and those lifeless eyes staring back at me will remain with me forever.

Later that afternoon I loaded Ponce's body along with the other dead onto a helicopter to be taken away. I watched that helicopter disappear into the sky carrying those dead men. Along with the death destruction and violence of which I have been apart, a part of me has also died. But from Ponce's death a new facet of me has been born. From my friend's death I have learned how to cry.

The Present Day—

Two days before that time my platoon was 29 men strong, the strongest field strength we ever had. That evening there was eleven of us left: battered, bewildered, shocked. It took two decades to understand and comprehend the inferno into which I had descended: the animal which I had become. There is a beast that lives deep within all of us and with some it lurks just beneath the surface. I live each day of my life struggling not so much with the moral dilemma of having killed but with the knowledge that I am capable of doing it. There is but one act that can rival the futility of taking life and that is the joy of giving life—the birth of my two children. Love, Chuck

CHARLIE'S ROAD TO RECOVERY BY CHARLIE DEPPEN

Reflecting on significant events from the past (wedding day, the birth of a child, an accident, or a significant sports team win or loss), we can recall everything in great detail as if viewing a video recording. That wasn't the way I recall the events surrounding my own experiences related to August 15, 1969 and the following time. I remember those events as a disconnected series of snapshots or video shorts.

Our platoon was part of a sweep through a ville, and my squad came up to a small dry ditch or ravine with an open field on the other side. The squad approached a bridge or path over the ditch to my left and then spread out. I moved to the far right of the squad.

I moved into a dry bed and up the other side on the field edge. Standing and ready to move across the field a shock-wave stunned and deafened me. Coming to my senses, I was numb and still standing on the edge of the field. I believe an explosion occurred.

I assessed my physical state by looking at my body. First, I understood I was alive and standing in the aftermath of an explosion. I checked my left and right arms and hands seeing no blood or wounds. Checking for blood I wiped a hand across by face. No blood!

Next, I looked at my left leg. Everything OK. Then I scanned my right leg, and I saw a piece of gray metal the size of a few nickels stacked together sticking out of my right kneecap. This surprised me. I felt no pain (In shock?), but I knew that piece of shrapnel didn't belong in my knee. I sat behind the ditch and called for a medic.

I cannot remember who came to my aid or how long I stood there. They placed me in an APC; the door was open. I think I was sitting or lying on the back right section. At least one other wounded soldier next to me, maybe more. Being in shock I didn't recognize him. What I remembered or focused on he appeared covered by debris from bamboo or bushes. My whole awareness of his condition became focused on a single piece of dirt and debris on his hand. His finger appeared broken at the joint and bent at a right angle. I thought how strange I only remember that specific injury. He could have many more serious injuries.

I had no sense of time passing. The next snapshot I am being helped on the dust-off for evacuation. I assumed I was the last wounded loaded because of my insignificant injury. No blood. No ill effects, except that pesky piece of shrapnel and a concussion. As my turn came, I felt relief I was leaving the battlefield. The helicopter took off and I was sitting up and thought it cool to look at the countryside passing below me as we flew away.

I don't remember landing or being taken into the operating theater, but I remember lying by myself inside and near the wall of what appeared a large tent. I watched doctors working on someone on the other side of the tent. It became my turn and I recall being annoyed they wanted to cut my right boot off before working on me. What a waste of a good boot!

They finished doing what they needed to do, and I made a mistake I regretted for over forty years. One person attending me offered me the piece of shrapnel that had been in my knee. I declined the offer. What a schmuck!

The next day (I guess) I found myself in a recovery ward with a large bandage wrapped around my right knee. A doctor told me the shrapnel hit a bulls-eye on my right kneecap, fracturing it. The aids periodically squirted fluid into the wound to rinse it out. After five days, they told me I had developed, what I understood, to be a Staph infection. I would need to be evacuated from Nam to Japan for surgery and follow-up treatment. It appeared my war was over for good.

I remember being visited by platoon members while in the medical ward; I guess in Duc Pho (but I could be wrong of the location). I don't remember who the visitors were. The Brigade commander visited, making rounds of the wards and handing out Zippos with the 11th Brigade emblem on one side and a map of Viet Nam on the other. I provided photos of the lighter to the 1st Platoon website.

They transferred me to Cam Ran Bay preparatory to my Golden Dust-off to Japan. I flew from Nam to Kishine Japan on August 22, 1969, my 23rd birthday. Best birthday present I ever got! Checking me into the orthopedic wing at Kishine (known as Kishine Barracks), a corpsman asked me my Date of Birth (DOB). I said "Today." He thought I was being a wise-ass (which I guess I was, in a way).

I settled into what I called an orthopedic wing of the hospital. Of the wounded I had the least serious wound. I must confess to severe survival guilt based on those assessments since I served with the First Platoon for only two and a half months. I am not aware a member of my platoon who left the unit for any reason in better health than I did. I got a 'million dollar wound'. This feeling of embarrassment at my good fortune increased due to the injuries of the other soldiers around me in Kishine. One young man in a bed near mine had lost both of his hands. A ward one floor below ours was for burn victims. Their prognosis and recoveries were grim. My experiences confirmed this being near them later as we were undergoing physical therapy. These reminders of the real costs to life and limb of war was one or my worst experiences from combat and its aftermath.

While in Japan, I received the first of my several operations. The doctor determined that the patella (kneecap) needed to be removed, and the tendons and sinews around the area re-routed/attached. The surgeon used a larger gauge for the drainage lines into and out of my knee (for delivery of antibiotics and draining of any fluid buildup). I think he experimented on me, but not sure. It may have contributed to my less than stellar recovery of motion during post-op.

After a month in Japan, the doctors transferred me to Fort Gordon, Georgia to continue recovery. My parents drove up from Tampa, Florida to meet the medical evacuation plane at Fort Gordon. There I received corrective surgery to increase my range of motion in my right knee. I had more physical therapy, including hydro-therapy in a swimming pool, which I found very helpful.

After a few months of recuperation at Fort Gordon, I got a short leave to go home to Tampa for Christmas. I got orders to report for duty to an armored company of the 1st Armored Division at Fort Hood, Texas on January 2nd. While there, I was standing at attention at an awards presentation on a parade ground and after I short time I fainted. They sent me to the hospital at Fort Hood for evaluation, and my Doctor got pissed off that they returned me to active duty with my poor state of recovery and underlying condition. He ordered a last round of surgeries and PT and then returned me to duty. It was with a profile: No running, jumping, stooping, bending, prolonged standing, or marching. I couldn't be given guard duty, KP, or any other special duty. The only duty I had after that was overnight CQ (Charge of Quarters). The Army transferred me into Supply and changed my MOS from 11B to 76Y. I became the company Supply Sergeant. That was my position until my Expiration of Term of Service (ETS) and discharge in early December, 1970.

TOMMY'S ROAD TO RECOVERY BY TOMMY THOMPSON

Sometimes it's yesterday. Most times its yesteryear. Flashback to that day that yesteryear. We were on patrol, working with Track-Asses (APCs). Having cleared a village, we moved across a clearing. Our point man held up a hand. Halt. I am on his right flank.

By the time he raised his hand, a loud explosion.

All hell broke loose.

A slow hell.

With the force of an Oklahoma tornado, the blast jerked me upward, skyward.

It happened so fast, yet it unfolded in slow motion.

The ground rose to meet me with a violent strike. A Joe Frazier gut punch.

I staggered to my feet. My right hand reached for the source of the piercing pain.

My fingers found the wound and my eyes found the blood. I fell. In slow motion.

The last thing I remembered was the crack of bullets being fired and exploding RPG rounds.

It was a blur. A fade to black.

As my senses came back, although only partially, I found myself on a stretcher, being hustled along at a slow speed. The soldiers carrying the stretcher slid it into the APC with other wounded platoon members. The APC with the wounded moved to a landing zone for the dust-off. Inside the APC, someone said, "You are going home."

Four words. They still ring in my ears a half-century later. Sometimes it's yesterday. We were still taking fire as the dust-off landed.

Once in the air, still struggling to understand, I wanted to grab the door gunner's foot, wanting him to shove it against my side for compression. I couldn't reach. I pointed to my side and his boot. He didn't know what I asked. And he was doing his job.

Once at the Chu Lai hospital medics put our stretchers on saw horses. Panic or pain, I had a hard time breathing. Extremely hard time. The reality and fear enveloped my brain, my senses, my being. The reality and fear of my wounds hit me and the realization I might not see home again.

After medics cut off my fatigues, they pushed me through the doors to another room. My feet hit the doors first, and the pain was excruciating. Damn, that hurt. I then saw my right foot had a through and through wound. And my brain let the rest of my body know, in no uncertain terms.

Before long, my attention shifted from my feet to my head. I grabbed for something being lifted from covering my nose and mouth. The oxygen cup. I was in the ICU. Please, I need that oxygen, soothing, cool. It felt so good, so comforting, I fought unseen forces to get it back.

At one point, thankful, I slept. Not a restful sleep. A fitful sleep. In one, I was back with my squad and under attack. The nightmare was real; I guess. I crawled out of bed and tumbled to the floor. Nurse and orderlies help me back in bed.

Our Brigade Commander came by to check on the wounded. He said two 250-pound bombs, booby-trapped to hit our tracks exploded. He gave me an 11th Brigade cigarette lighter. I don't know whatever became of it. Two years ago, I learned it was Colonel Jack Treadwell. His family lived in the same town as my dad's family in Snyder, Oklahoma. There was a monument to him in a park that bears his name in Snyder.

I had no memory being moved to Cam Rahn Bay from Chu Lai. It was a blur then. Time still had not brought it into full focus.

But I recall the C141 trip from Cam Rahn to Tachikawa Air Force Base in Japan. We were on stretchers, attached to a metal framework stacked four or five high on both sides along the center in the guts of our air taxi ride. Once unloaded and carried inside to the air base hospital, we remained for two days. I remember a beautiful blonde nurse who exhibited compassion for the wounded under her care. Her compassion was the last I would see, or felt, for years to come. Wish I could remember her name.

After three days I took a bumpy ride in an M*A*S*H-like bus, still on a stretcher, through the streets of Yokohama to Kishine. Funny, I don't remember seeing any sights along the way. Must have been on the bottom.

There are bad memories and good memories of my stay at the 106th.

Bad first. I had two infections develop during the first week. One was at the bottom of the incision running the length of my chest to my belly button. The second was the top right part of my right foot. The infection on my foot happened first. Stitches on the inside of my foot below the ankle had to be removed. They cleaned my open wounds each day. Think of hellfire and brimstone. The infection above my belly button was kindred to half of a small rubber ball of puss. It had to be opened. I swear they didn't deaden the wound as they opened it. I tried to punch the doctor, or whatever he was, but the nurse saw my reaction and grabbed my right arm. My red-hair temper came to light. The timing wasn't good. Now, I had three open wounds. They stitched the wounds again once they contained the infection.

Then there was the laxative incident. I got into a wheelchair and able to wheel to the mess hall, bathroom, etc. Without getting graphic, let's say the laxative worked. It worked too well. Too fast. I didn't make it to the bathroom. As one might imagine, I wasn't popular with the nurse or the orderlies.

But enough of the bad. Let's remember the good.

Coming back from a particular physical-therapy session, I saw the bottom half of my bed stacked with mail and a big package. It was September, and the first mail I received since late July. I had many letters to read. No better feeling for a Grunt than mail from home. After reading, and re-reading, every letter, I asked if I could call home. It had to be a collect call. Interacting with Japanese telephone operators wasn't too terrible.

My wife, Connie, answered, it was so incredible. The best feeling in the world. She didn't know I would be calling. Besides that, it was 3 o'clock in the morning in Bristow, Oklahoma. Don't remember too much of our talk. But I know there were tears and many "I love you's."

I lost weight during this ordeal. I had little weight to lose. One of the weirdest things brought to us was beer. We received beer three times a day. During one of those times I had Stag beer. I didn't like it. Still don't drink it today. Even if they still make it. (I hope they don't.) The guy in the bed next to me had a Presbyterian minister visiting him. The minister kept looking at the beer on my food tray. I asked him if he wanted the beer since I didn't want it. He took the beer and drank it. Blew me away.

The cinema and PX was across the hospital compound so using a wheelchair was a chore. The first movie was 'Support Your Local Sheriff,' the comedy-action film starring Oklahoma's own James Garner. It felt good to laugh out loud. To this day, it still is in my top ten movie list.

The flight back stateside.

The buses took us back to Tachikawa, still on stretchers, and again carried onto a C141. There was a small city of us wounded, stacked and lining the middle of the transport. I recall there was wounded sitting on both sides in those strap-type seats. We left Japan around noon on a Tuesday and arrived at Travis Air Base in Oakland at 5 am Tuesday.

They carried us to a building and set us on a concrete floor. They brought a tray of food loaded with steak and eggs, pancakes, and much more. Couldn't eat a bite. We could call home too. What a blessing to be on U.S. soil and tell your wife you are safe.

After a brief stay in Brooke Army Hospital, San Antonio, they transferred me to Oklahoma at Ft. Sill. Back at last. Connie and one of my best friends, Barry West, and his wife, drove to Lawton to see me.

Gee, good to be back home again.

Sometimes it seemed like yesterday.

REFLECTION—AUGUST 16

I woke early and sat by my gear, having a cigarette, thinking of the last couple of days and wondering how Mike was doing. I hadn't slept well and kept running through the names of everyone in the platoon who'd died since I'd arrived at the platoon: "Tufts, Ramos, Reynolds, Jerry, Swindle, Wellman, Ponce, Mitchell, Anderson, and Carey." It was as if I did this so I would never forget them. It worked. Some nights a squad member would wake me up because I was reciting the names out loud in my sleep, and they feared it might attract the enemy.

Lieutenant Baxter stopped by and asked, "Haynie, how are you doing?"

I replied, "I am OK, Sir."

After he left, I thought of the action we'd endured the last three days. I tried to understand why it was so different than any other earlier action. Action on the 13th was close and personal. The enemy was so close that I will never forget their facial expressions or the bullets I fired that riddled their bodies. The enemy fired their weapons and tried to kill us at a much closer range. They stayed and fought longer and harder than in any other engagement. We'd had earlier actions where we had mostly fought at a distance. We fired hundreds to thousands of rounds at the enemy at a greater distance. They fired back with as many rounds to answer us and then fled. Or snipers or small units engaged us and then ran while we opened fire and chased them. Or sappers closed in on our positions throwing explosive charges and fired automatic weapons under the cover of darkness. None of it had been as intense as the last three days. Hard to reason or explain.

I tried to figure if I could have done anything different to spot the ambushes earlier. Being the point man, it was my responsibility to give the platoon an early warning of danger. I'm out front to protect the platoon.

What if, on the 13th, I hadn't crossed the trench to engage the enemy but warned the platoon and stayed on our side of the trench? Would the enemy have allowed us to move through without firing on us? If they had opened fire, would we have been prepared and not caught by surprise at their strength and firepower? Did I get Jerry, Swindle, and Rebel killed by opening fire on the enemy first?

What if, on the 15th, I had taken a different route by moving the platoon to the left or right of the large hedgerow to my front when I sensed danger? Why didn't I yell, "Hit the ground!" instead of yelling, "Spread out?" If we had hit the ground, would Mitchell, Ponce, Anderson, and Carey have survived?

Would the platoon have trusted me to walk point again? Did they blame me? I continued to run the 13th and 15th through my mind for years and years. I needed a different outcome.

I glanced downward at my shirt, and the left side had bloodstains. The blood might have been from Brown, as I held his head against me, or it may have been Jerry's blood as I rolled him into my arms. My (Ponce's) M-16 came in view, and, picking it up, I found blood covering the left side. I got my canteen of water and an undershirt, and rubbed as hard as possible to remove the blood. I felt the two grenades I'd found beside Jerry in my side shirt pocket. Pulling the grenades out, I noticed that they were covered in blood and other human matter, as was the inside of my pocket. I broke and cried. I realized that I hadn't had time to mourn Jerry, Rebel, Swindle, and Frank before now.

Once I regained my composure, I picked up the two grenades, my entrenching tool, and two cans of fruit, and moved to the edge of the perimeter. Chuck Council was on guard. We made eye contact and nodded to each other. I found a good location to the right of a path and dug a hole 18 inches deep. I placed the two grenades in the hole with the handles up and the pins facing the side of the hole; then I packed dirt around them and placed a can of fruit on each one to put weight on the grenade handle. Carefully, I pulled the pin from each grenade and finished packing dirt on top, leaving a mound so it was noticeable. I told Jerry, Rebel, Frank, and

Swindle that soon they would get even. After returning to my position, I got out my soap and water and washed the blood off my hands and tried to scrub the blood out of my uniform. I had to wear the uniform another four days. I carried Ponce's M-16 the rest of my time in the field.

It was on this day that I lost my faith in God. I know many soldiers find God in combat, but I could not continue to believe. I was Methodist. Growing up, I went to church, and I considered myself a Christian. The death and suffering I'd seen the last couple of months had convinced me there was no merciful deity watching over us. How could there be, seeing how 19- and 20-year-old sons, fathers, and husbands had died or were wounded? If God exists, I hated him! I felt no remorse for taking a human life; it was kill or be killed. Mike said earlier it wasn't personal. Now it was personal! I could think only of killing gooks.

I decided that it was only Mike and the rest of First Platoon keeping me safe; no one else would answer if I called out. Mike would! I wished Mike was there; the blast shook him. With any luck, he didn't have a serious injury and would be returning soon.

Later I learned that a festival called Woodstock, billed as "Three Days of Peace & Music," had started August 15 and was occurring as we loaded dust-off helicopters with the dead and wounded. I felt bitter, thinking some were probably draft dodgers or most didn't give a damn about us. They danced, sang, and partied while my friends got killed or wounded and I was in the jungles of Vietnam. I thought it would be great if they'd come to Vietnam; then our platoon size would not be half the allowed strength. Some sincerely protested the war in Vietnam. But my instincts tell me most were protesting the war because *they* didn't want to go to Vietnam as *individuals*; they didn't care about the politics of the war. Big difference. They wanted peace but didn't want to serve. More than 400,000 attended Woodstock. What if 400,000 young people came together to support us?

This is a letter from Charlie Deppen to his mother and father, dated August 16, 1969.

Dear Mom and Dad,

    Don't worry about me since I'm almost perfectly all right. I say almost because yesterday our company was operating in the Quang Ngai valley and our platoon got ambushed. They (the NVA) blew a mine and I caught a little shrapnel in the right knee, but it's not too serious. I got dusted off real fast and now this wound will keep me out of the field for a while and maybe permanently. It's possible that the knee cap is slightly fractured, but I can still get around on my own. At least I'll have lots of time to read and to organize my bridge system.

    Be cool and don't worry about me. I'm much safer here than in the field.

    Love Charlie

During the next three days, two helicopters got shot down, and one tank ran over a 250-pound bomb booby trap. Mike, Alabama, and Bill Davenport were back with the platoon. On August 20, Lieutenant Baxter told me to get on the resupply chopper to go back to Bronco. I was still nauseous and dizzy, and I was experiencing severe headaches, blurred vision, and ringing in my ears. Once we landed, I checked in with the First Sergeant, and he dispatched a jeep to take me to the hospital. The driver dropped me off at the entrance and left. I entered the hospital and stood at the entrance, not knowing where to go. A medic saw me standing near the entrance, looking confused.

He asked, "Do you need help?"

I replied, "I was near an explosion several days ago, and I'm still feeling sick and unstable."

He said, "Follow me." I followed the medic to his desk and sat in a chair facing him.

He asked, "What is your unit?"

I told him "Alpha Company, 3rd of the 1st." The medic found and pulled out my medical records from a file drawer.

He asked, "What happened? Give me details."

143

I stated, "I was near an explosion, and my heart and breathing stopped; Owens gave me CPR. I was unconscious for a while. I'm still nauseous. I have severe headaches, blurred vision, and ringing in both ears." He recorded that information, took my vitals, and then sent me into an open room with a bed.

Five minutes later a doctor came in, and we had the same conversation. I guess it was difficult for the medics and doctors because I had no penetrating wound to be treated. A mild brain injury didn't exist in the triage of Vietnam, and it was not considered a Traumatic Brain Injury (TBI) without a penetrating wound. The doctor said they didn't have the diagnostic equipment needed and sent me to the Division Hospital at Chu Lai.

A truck took five of us and several medics to the airfield to board the next flight to Chu Lai. I felt embarrassed because they were far worse off than me. Once we landed, a bus took me and the other wounded and medics to the hospital. After we'd arrived, a doctor treated me and held me overnight for observation. He diagnosed me with a concussion, vertigo, and tinnitus from my proximity to the August 15 explosion. No special test was given. Years later, the doctors diagnosed me with a TBI resulting from the explosion. The next morning they sent me back to Bronco, and I remained at company headquarters for several days' bed rest, which meant I had no duty and was to stay in bed. I was ready to return to the platoon and did the morning of August 24.

This is an excerpt from a letter Lieutenant John Baxter wrote to his parents on August 21, 1969.

"Well two days to stand down & we are ready for it. The platoon is tired after some hard 14 days in the field. Also I should get a few breaks myself. Stand down is 24 Aug to 27 . . . then week of pay officer, then 9 to 16 Sept I should have in-country leave somewhere. My out of the field date is still undetermined late Sept or Oct. I'll be looking for a job in Chu Lai. The rumors of withdrawal, deactivation of the 11th LIB and "lull" in the war continue. However enemy pressure continues . . . harassing type operations with no other objective than killing & injuring GI's. . . . The VC fire 6 to 8 rounds hoping to hit somebody then run because they know arty barrages will follow. Only once in many such attacks has anybody been hurt. Also replacements are still coming . . . I'm now the 2nd most senior plt ldr in the battalion. So it can't be too long.

Tomorrow is the last day of stand down and again I'm in charge of the awards ceremony. However few company awards have cleared yet. I have put two of my SP4's in for Silver Stars but I'll be gone before they are awarded.

Not too much more to talk about from this vantage point. Life gets to a routine & conversations mean little to anyone except us in the field."

August 24. The company was back on the Hill. Later that same morning, the platoon loaded into a Chinook helicopter and departed to Chu Lai for stand-down. Once we'd landed, the rear door lowered. We moved out of the helicopter toward the containers for storage of our weapons and ammunition. It felt strange turning in your weapon, ammunition, grenades, and claymore mines for the three days while on stand-down. I felt defenseless. I kept my knife.

We moved into a building that had one large room that contained stacked bunk beds and lockers. We choose our bunks and locker to store the rest of our gear. Mike and I grabbed a bunk, him on the lower bunk and me on the upper. We sat on his bunk and talked a while about going to the hospital and our return to the platoon. We never talked about what happened during those three days. The mood was solemn and the platoon members quiet. I remember no one talking about those days. If a platoon member brought it up he said, "Do you remember the 13th, or do you remember the 15th?" We understood what they were talking about regardless of the current month. And that was all we said.

I wasn't in the partying mood during this stand-down. I stayed on my bunk reading and sleeping, and I drank too much Jim Beam and Coke. I found a couple western paperback books and stashed them under my pillow to read while here. The only time I left my bunk was to eat and to listen to a band one evening. I even passed up the continuous poker games and going to the enlisted club during this stand-down.

The three days passed quickly, and before you knew it, we picked up our weapons and the rest of our gear and loaded into the helicopters. We flew back to the Hill.

Once we landed and departed the helicopter, Lieutenant Baxter called the platoon over to his location and told us we would stay on the Hill for the day to receive training. He said we would go through three training stations: squad fire and maneuver, first aid, and calling in artillery. This announcement surprised us because we never received formal training. I thought this training late after the last couple of weeks.

As the two squads separated to go to the training stations, Lieutenant Baxter said, "Dankert and Haynie, stay here." Mike and I looked at each other, wondering if we were in trouble.

He walked toward us and said, "I have something for you two" as he reached into his shirt pocket and pulled out sergeant pins.

He said, "Dankert and Haynie, you are promoted to Acting Sergeant." Then he handed us the sergeant pins.

Lieutenant Baxter shook our hands and said, "Well deserved."

We thanked Lieutenant Baxter for his confidence in us and at once pinned on our stripes. We both felt proud of the promotion and that Lieutenant Baxter had been the one to recognize us.

Mike and I received a promotion to Specialist Fourth Class the middle of August. We never wore that rank. An Acting Sergeant had the authority and responsibility of the rank but not the pay. We wouldn't be officially promoted to Sergeant until the middle of November. After we returned to our squad, our squad members noticed the sergeant stripes on our collars. We received good-natured ribbing for the rest of the afternoon. They were happy for us.

We thought the first-aid training was valuable and wished we'd had this training several weeks earlier. They covered how to handle a casualty of an explosion—like what had happened to me—and Sergeant Owens performed what should be done. Calling in artillery was challenging and fun. We got to use our map-reading and radio skills for this part of the training. Not too difficult. The fire-and-maneuver training wasn't realistic, and we gave the poor sergeant teaching this phase of training a hard time.

After we'd completed the training and had a hot meal at the mess hall, the platoon prepared to move off the Hill. We patrolled the area around the horseshoe and then moved to the mountains because of the monsoon season.

LETTERS FROM DUSTY

One evening as we finished our dinner meal, Lieutenant Baxter called over most of the platoon to his location. He thanked us for coming over and told us he'd received two letters from Dusty Rhoades. Lieutenant Baxter opened the first letter and read out loud to the platoon members gathered around him. He then opened the second letter and read it to the platoon. Dusty's letters told us he was in the states and doing well. The platoon felt relief that Dusty was healing.

We seldom heard from or knew what happened to our wounded platoon members. At the end of the second letter Dusty asked about Joe Mitchell, Paul Ponce, and Ryan Okino and how they were doing and to write him back. You can sense the sadness that overcame the platoon members. Lieutenant Baxter asked who wanted to respond to Dusty and said he would give them his address. No one spoke. I didn't want to tell Dusty what happened on August 13 and 15. Mike didn't, either. I thought if he didn't know maybe he could heal faster and move on with his life thinking they were alive. To my knowledge, no one wrote Dusty.

The platoon had received replacements before the three-day stand-down and several more after we'd returned to the field. We had many new people assigned to the platoon in late August and early September, replacing those killed and wounded August 13 and 15. As usual, most were 20-year-old draftees from across the United States. Battalion diverted many replacements from Bravo Company. The replacements I remember were Donald Ayres, Allyn Buff (see Appendix F), Cliff Sivadge, James Thornton, Terry Woolums (see appendix G), David Kingsbury, John Conti, Manuel Strauch, Archie Oliver, Michael Hardman, David Abernathy, and Wilbert Teaberry.

This is an excerpt from a letter Lieutenant John Baxter wrote to his parents August 29, 1969.

Came to Bronco tonight to be pay officer. Your package of 13 August arrived in good shape; many thanks. . . . like to have another package of small cans of vegetables. They really improve the C's. . . . Send more. We got a new platoon leader today. So I am the next to be replaced under the normal replacement system . . . A quiet night tonight.

Figure 34 Jack Lanzer on break outside Hill 4-11. Photo provided by Mike Dankert.

Figure 35 Glyn Haynie ready for mission on August 13, 1969. Photo provided by Glyn Haynie.

Figure 36 Chuck Council ready for mission August 13, 1969. Photo provided by Glyn Haynie.

Figure 37 Mike Dankert with APC named "The Rolling Stones" on FSB 4-11. Bumper sticker says "Give Peace a Chance" WKNR 13 (Detroit radio station.) Photo provided by Mike Dankert.

Figure 38 SSG Robert Swindle KIA August 13, 1969. Photo provided by John Baxter.

Figure 39 Jerry Ofstedahl (KIA August 13, 1969.) Picture taken on FSB Debbie.

Figure 40 Richard "Rebel" Wellman KIA August 13, 1969. Photo provided by Brenda Jones (Rebel's sister).

Figure 41 Joe Mitchell (KIA August 15, 1969) Basic Training photo.

Figure 42 James Anderson (KIA August 15, 1969) Basic Training photo.

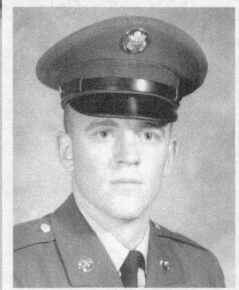

Figure 43 Danny Carey (KIA August 15, 1969) Basic Training photo.

Figure 44 Paul Ponce (KIA August 15, 1969) walking to Hill 4-11 first day. Photo provided by Charlie Deppen and photo taken by Steve Tippon, *Southern Cross Newspaper.*

Figure 45 Tommy Thompson (WIA August 15, 1969) Basic Training picture. Photo provided by Tommy Thompson.

152

Figure 46 Ryan Okino (WIA August 15, 1969) walking to Hill 4-11 July 8, 1969. Photo provided by Charlie Deppen and photo taken by Steve Tippon, *Southern Cross Newspaper.*

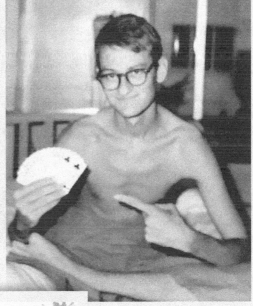

Figure 47 Charlie Deppen (WIA August 15, 1969) in hospital in Japan. Photo provided by Charlie Deppen.

Figure 48 Mike Dankert standing (WIA August 15, 1969) and Bill Davenport, sitting (WIA August 15, 1969); returned to field after August 15, 1969. Photo provided by Mike Dankert.

CHANGES

September was a pivotal month for Mike and me as we assumed added responsibilities. During this month, Captain Tyson and Lieutenant Baxter would leave the company for other assignments. Chuck Council, Alabama, Sergeant Owens, and Maurice Harrington would leave for rear jobs. We had been with the platoon only four months, in Vietnam for six months, but now, we were the old-timers. Many new replacements arrived. They needed to be watched over and trained. And this included officers.

Mike and I became the informal leaders within the platoon. There were periods Mike and I filled in at leadership positions—squad leader, platoon sergeant, and platoon leader—within the platoon. We had "shake-n-bake" NCO's; they outranked us and were assigned to leadership positions. They attended an eight-week course, Non-commissioned Officer Candidate Course (NCOCC), after AIT and were promoted to Sergeant upon graduation. So they arrived in Vietnam and to the platoon with two months of extra classroom instruction. Unlike the soldiers they led, most had no combat experience.

I became withdrawn and angry and had a hard time accepting the things I saw and did in Vietnam, especially the events of August 13 and August 15. Up to this point, we'd had 10 platoon members killed and 11 platoon members wounded. Seven of the wounded went back stateside. We received no official information whether they'd lived or died. No training prepared me for this. How could a 19-year-old rationalize people, his friends, his brothers, dying or being wounded in such horrific ways? If something happened, we said "It don't mean nothing," as if this excused us from having any feelings. I turned off my emotions.

I was hard on the new guys, not wanting them to die or get injured. Nor did I want to know them. This was not a conscious decision; it just happened. With no formal leadership training, using only my combat experiences and instincts, I did my best to share and teach the FNGs how to survive. Mike's training methods showed more patience and understanding.

As we received replacements, Mike and I did a quick evaluation by watching and listening to the FNGs. Cliff Sivadge stood out among the replacements. He arrived early to mid-September. Cliff was from Iowa, taller than me, and weighed more; he had black hair and was easy-going but serious if needed. He didn't act like someone who didn't need training. He was pleasant and quick to join a conversation.

You'd be surprised how many new guys came into the platoon with a swagger, and you couldn't teach them. Cliff blended into the platoon well. We thought he might make a team leader or squad leader one day. Mike and I made him our understudy. We concentrated on teaching him the fundamentals of survival in the field and combat. Cliff was a fast learner and absorbed the information, wanting more. We felt good about our choice.

I selected another replacement, Terry Woolums, to learn how to walk point and how to enter and exit tunnels. Terry was my height, weighing 140 pounds. He had brown hair; he was 20 years old and from Decatur,

Illinois. He arrived at the platoon in late August. Terry was talkative and walked with a swagger as if he didn't need training. It wasn't cool for an FNG to act this way, but I assumed Terry was doing this to hide his lack of confidence. I had a gut instinct he would be good at the job, and he expressed an interest.

I showed him how to avoid booby traps, look for evidence of NVA or VC movement, and which trail to use or not use. Several times I found and pointed out booby traps, and his first instinct was to touch or try to disarm them. This made me nervous and not as trustful with him up front. I showed him how to mark its location or destroy it in place, depending on our location or type of booby trap. He didn't want to enter tunnels. I believe I convinced him one time to go into a tunnel. His first experience entering a tunnel was with no contact with the enemy, but he never entered a tunnel again. I started to doubt my choice.

My memories of the people and events during the months following August are vague, not as sharp as my first six months in-country. I am not sure if this was because of my injury on the 15th or if I'd quit trying to remember. Possibly it was both. Most of the enemy contact for the next couple months was lighter, with us dealing with booby traps, snipers, and small units. Nothing compared to the earlier months! Maybe going to the mountains had been a good thing. Maybe the enemy thought so, too. Hell, the mountains and monsoons could be your enemy, too!

QUANG NGAI CITY

During the five and half months we worked on and off Hill 4-11, we went into Quang Ngai City only twice that I remember. The first time Mike and I volunteered to pull security for the APCs that were going into the city for a resupply run for fuel, ice, beer, and soda. We met the APCs outside the Hill entrance, did the introductions, and climbed aboard for the ride. We sat to the left and right of the main gunner, watching the road for booby traps and scouring the tree line for possible ambush sites. Mike and I chatted with the crew members and tried to pass the time for the ride. The ride into the city was uneventful.

We transitioned from the dirt road to a paved road as we got closer to the city. Within minutes, we entered the city. It was strange to see Vietnamese walking along streets going to work, couples together on a walk, or women shopping for the dinner meal. It appeared so normal. There were many shops open and outside markets selling household and food items. As we passed the pedestrians and shoppers, they looked up and smiled. I knew that smile, and it wasn't real. I didn't sense being welcomed but smiled back. Children ran behind the APC shouting and waving, most asking for chop-chop (food).

The APCs left Mike and me at an NCO club until they were ready to head back to the Hill. I think that the NCO club was a Military Assistance Command Vietnam (MAC-V) club that supported a MAC-V unit that worked from Quang Ngai, but I could be wrong. It was not a large club, but, to us, it was plush. It had overstuffed, red-leather chairs and several booths covered with the same red leather. The tables had shiny wooden tops.

A Vietnamese female bartender who spoke good English was tending bar. On duty, we couldn't drink alcohol, so we ordered Cokes. She served us a refreshing ice-cold Coke. We seldom had any ice-cold beverages. We sat there being quiet, enjoying the air-conditioning and the cold Cokes. The bartender engaged in conversation, but I thought she wasn't interested in us or what we had to say but was only practicing her English. This was fine with me because I enjoyed hearing a woman talk for a change.

Ready to leave, the track commander sent someone to get us, and we loaded up to head back to the Hill. We headed out of the city, taking the dirt road for our uneventful drive back. As we drove past the first bunker on the Hill, I acknowledged how primitive our "city" was compared to Quang Ngai City.

The second time into Quang Ngai, Captain Tyson tasked the platoon with providing security around the Quang Ngai airfield. I don't remember why the airfield needed security that night in particular. I can only assume that the command had intelligence that something was likely to happen. We expected the mission to be easy and thought of it as a nice change of pace.

We received orders of the mission as the platoon was working the foothills of the mountains. The platoon created a landing zone for the helicopters coming to pick us up and fly us to the airfield. A platoon member popped smoke and guided the three helicopters to the landing zone. They landed, and the platoon members climbed aboard their assigned helicopter. Once loaded, the helicopters lifted off and headed to the airfield. The flight took ten minutes, and the helicopters landed on the airfield. We jumped off and moved away from the helicopters as they departed.

We established our positions around the airfield and made sure we had good fields of fire. The tree line was several hundred meters away, so our visibility was good. The enemy needed to travel a distance without concealment to get to us. We settled in before nightfall and had our dinner meal. We established the guard rotation and sat around talking, reading, or relaxing until the sun slid down below the horizon.

As the sun was dropping below the horizon, we saw figures approaching from the city side of our position. As they got closer, we determined they were ARVN soldiers (the good guys) with women. Once they got to our position, they offered to sell their wives for the evening. An ARVN looked at our squad, pointed at his wife, and said "Boom-boom five dollar." "Boom-boom" in Vietnam meant "to have sex." The women didn't appear they wanted any part of what their husbands offered. None of us were against having women around, but we found it distasteful for a man to be selling his wife. You had to draw the line somewhere from the insanity of this war. We rounded up the three or four ARVN soldiers and the wives and made them leave the airfield. I guess the ARVN command didn't think the airfield was a security risk, or ARVN soldiers with their wives wouldn't have been roaming the airfield.

The night passed without incident. We woke the next morning and had breakfast. After breakfast we packed our gear and waited for our transportation back to the mountains. At mid-day, we boarded the Hueys and flew back to the foothills west of the Hill.

GOING TO DA NANG

Our platoon was back patrolling the foothills west of firebase 4-11 and below the mountains. We moved through a ville to search for enemy soldiers, food, supplies, and weapons. The Quang Ngai province had always been an NVA/VC stronghold, and our expectations were to be cautious around the civilian population, especially going into a village. Once in a village, it was common practice to move the village population into a centralized location so we could make sure that if we encountered anyone, we didn't mistake them for a friendly. Whatever a friendly might be.

Moving the villagers, I noticed the normal population of old men, old women, and women with small children. We seldom found teenage or adult males in a village. Adding to the chaos, we had to avoid the ever-present animals running around the village. We needed to search 40 huts, which takes time.

We broke into two-man teams and moved from hut to hut searching for any item that might aid the enemy. Bill Davenport and I formed up as a team. We looked for signs of equipment, weapons, or food hidden underground inside or near a hut. Bill and I moved among the huts searching around and between them. We searched food bins and storage for livestock feed and looked for entrances to tunnels that might connect to VC or NVA soldiers.

Clearing a village was hot, slow, and nerve-wracking. The platoon was on edge. We didn't want to piss off the civilian populace. We were careful how we handled the villagers and their belongings. As Bill and I moved from one hut to another, we stopped to search where a grass mat four by eight feet lay on the ground. We flipped the grass mat back and saw only dirt. It didn't look natural, so we kicked at what appeared to be the edges and found the dirt covered a cover. We requested another team to watch for movement as we lifted the covering and flipped it over, hoping to see no VC. To our surprise the hole was four feet deep and held 20 weapons: AK-47s, RPGs, old Springfield rifles, and plenty of ammunition. This was a good find. Lieutenant Baxter radioed in the weapons cache, and a helicopter soon arrived to retrieve the weapons and ammunition. Bill and I helped load the cache we found and watched the helicopter take flight back to Duc Pho.

We finished clearing the village and moved several klicks away to our night position near the river. Lieutenant Baxter called Bill and me over to the CP position and told us we'd received a three-day in-country R & R to Da Nang for discovering the weapons cache. Lieutenant Baxter made two soldiers happy. Clean clothes, hot showers, regular food, a bunk, and other enjoyments of life, here we come!

Bill and I caught the supply chopper back to FSB Bronco two days later for our three-day in-country R & R in Da Nang. The base in Da Nang was one of the largest in Vietnam and was secure; we would not have to worry about enemy attacks. We reported to the First Sergeant to get our orders and then headed to the supply room. Bill and I turned in our weapons and our gear to be secured during our absence. We both hated leaving our weapons behind, but that was the policy. The supply sergeant gave us clean uniforms, underclothes, and socks, and we headed to the shower room. We stripped and showered off weeks of dirt and sweat and put on our clean clothes.

Our flight to Da Nang boarded in an hour, so we got a ride to the airfield to wait for our flight. In a short time we boarded through the rear of the C-130 and dropped into empty seats. The ramp closed, and the C-130 began its taxi along the runway, gathering speed until the lumbering plane lifted off the ground. We both nodded off, and it wasn't long before we descended to approach the Da Nang airfield for landing. The descent was steep and fast, but the landing was smooth enough, considering it was a C-130.

Bill and I exited through the rear ramp and walked to the terminal. We checked in at the front desk, and the Marine NCO provided instructions for bus transportation and our quarters. We arrived at the Air Force part of the base and found out what many soldiers had never discovered. The Air Force knew how to live! Air Force quarters (living area) were large, clean, and comfortable, with a hooch girl, Vietnamese woman, assigned to keep your room clean. The best part was the mess hall; every meal had dozens of entrée choices and many desserts. Army mess halls never had this many food choices at any meal. I bet I put on five pounds in those three days; I sure could use it! Bill and I spent plenty of time at the mess hall. Each morning after breakfast we went to the massage parlor and received a steam bath, and got bathed and massaged. We went to movies. Bill and I went to the NCO club every night. We didn't even cause any trouble. The three days went by fast, and before we knew it, we were back at Duc Pho picking up our weapons and gear and waiting to catch a supply chopper back to the platoon.

Returning to the platoon, we found that Captain Kinney, a younger West Point graduate with far less experience, had replaced Captain Tyson. We respected Captain Tyson and didn't want him to leave.

CALLING IN ARTILLERY

The platoon was patrolling the foothills northwest of the Hill, not far from the river. As usual, there had been VC and NVA spotted in the AO. We got a report that Third Platoon was receiving sniper fire from outside a village half a klick from us. Our platoon, on the opposite side of the village, had a better view of the enemy than Third Platoon. Third platoon requested Lieutenant Baxter to call in artillery fire on the sniper's position. Their platoon leader thought there was more than one sniper firing at their position. Hitting the village with artillery rounds was a concern.

Lieutenant Baxter called Mike and me over to his position and said, "I want you two to move to a location 20 meters outside the village to figure where the sniper-fire location is. Then call in an artillery strike on the position."

Mike and I replied, "Yes, Sir" at the same time.

Lieutenant Baxter continued, "The platoon will stay in place for support." He handed me the map, and Mike got the radio from John Meyer, the Lieutenant's RTO.

Mike and I moved toward the village. We crawled through the low grass and thorns the last 50 feet to a location between two trees, using high underbrush for concealment. It offered an excellent vantage point of the village. We heard the distinct crack of AK-47s firing from the south side of the village and pinpointed their firing position. We had an excellent view of their position, but we could not see the soldiers who were firing. Our biggest fear was an artillery shell hitting the village. We needed to be damned exact calling in the fire mission.

The two of us lay behind the trees between the enemy's position and our platoon. Using the map, I marked the location, and Mike called in smoke for the first round. This made sure we called the artillery to the correct location, but this gave the enemy time to escape the HE rounds before they landed. The smoke round popped above where the sniper firing was coming from; we knew they were on target. I requested three HE rounds to the same grid coordinates. Mike relayed the information, and we waited. It seemed like a long time. The rounds came in one after another, exploding on target. The snipers didn't fire on Third Platoon again.

Mike and I moved back to the First Platoon location, and both of us had big grins. The training we'd gotten earlier had helped. We reported to Lieutenant Baxter that the three rounds hit the enemy position. Third Platoon reported back to Lieutenant Baxter that the rounds landed on target but that no enemy dead had been found.

LIEUTENANT BAXTER GETS A REAR JOB

Early to mid-September, Lieutenant Baxter got the word he was leaving the field for his rear job. He was going to the Battalion S-2 to be the battalion intelligence officer. It was normal for officers to spend six months in the field leading soldiers and then the last six months of their tour in a rear job. The Army tried to rotate officers so as many as possible could get combat experience. Lieutenant Baxter's leaving was a sad day for First Platoon.

He'd arrived to First Platoon in April 1969; he was 26 years old, had a college degree, and had served two years with the Peace Corps in Chile. After graduating Officer Candidate School (OCS), he'd attended the U.S. Army Jungle Operations Training before going to Vietnam. He had far more worldly experience than the average platoon leader and even some company commanders. Lieutenant Baxter proved to be an excellent officer. Most of the platoon members, if not all, respected and liked Lieutenant Baxter. He was intelligent and fair, and he led by example. We never thought about an order he gave—we did what he told us to do. We never knew him on a personal level because he kept everything professional, which worked well for the platoon. I am sure it did for him, as well; it was better not having close relationships with soldiers who may die or be wounded under his command. He didn't have the friendship or bond that we, the enlisted men, shared; he missed out on that.

Even after the losses of August 13 and 15, it was Lieutenant Baxter who'd kept the platoon together without key NCO leadership positions—platoon sergeant and squad leaders—being filled. He was always calm and reassuring; I can personally attest to the fact that this helped us to do our jobs with less fear. Whoever would replace Lieutenant Baxter would have a large pair of boots to fill. We would miss him.

This is an excerpt from a letter Lieutenant John Baxter wrote to his parents on September 11, 1969.

> I'm sitting on the patio of the Navy O Club overlooking the beautiful sand of S. China Sea. The sun is back out over I Corps after a 10 day absence. The first taste of the monsoon started at dawn on the first and it rained off & on for the next ten days. On the second I went back to the mountains with company and from the 2nd to 6th we searched for base camps & climbed hills 896,922 & 716(all in meters). Lots of humping but we saw nothing. On the

6th we went back to LZ4-11 for ten days. However, on the night of the eighth I went to Bronco to get ready for the in-country R&R. . . . All seems peaceful now with the truce. . . . Maybe Ho's death will let this thing die out but I really don't think so. Hopefully they'll keep Da Nang peaceful while I'm here. Though it is not a certainty it appears I'm out of the field for good now & will take the Battalion S-2 job. So it looks, happily, that my days as a rifle platoon leader are over.

Forty-Six years later, John Baxter wrote this comment to First Platoon on the platoon website about his time with the platoon:

So for a little over 5 months, 1st Platoon, A Company, 3rd Battalion, 1st Infantry had a 26-year-old lieutenant as its leader. While these letters home rekindled the memory of events 46 years ago, most of my vivid memories are scrambled. I can recall events but they are only snapshots and I am not sure I will ever put them together chronologically.

Reflecting 46 years later, those five months were a period of conflict between the futility of why are we doing this and the command pressure to kill as many of the enemy as possible because that was all that seemed to matter. My letters change over that period. The newness wears off and I sense being caught in the middle-take no casualties but kill. The reality is that the role of a rifle platoon leader is one of the loneliest jobs I can think of. I do not say this out of pity for me. I volunteered albeit under duress and took my chances. The platoon leader does not have the comradery the enlisted man has especially when the platoon operates alone. However, the nature of the Army is that officers are better off. We only had to stay in the field five to six months and you had to be there for most of your one-year tour. While we made mistakes on balance, we did the best we could. I will always be indebted to all of you for your support.

The first replacement Lieutenant, I don't remember his name, was overweight and soft. He was new to the Army and being an officer. We could tell he was not Lieutenant Baxter! This would be a hard transition. We had complete trust in Lieutenant Baxter to make sound decisions and to look out for our welfare. We were not confident with this Lieutenant.

He complained of everything; living conditions, being wet, food, water, long hours, being dirty, weather, and the humping. Now a soldier complaining was OK but not the Platoon Leader. In defense of the Lieutenant, I need to state he was a pharmacist or studying to be one before being drafted, if I remember correctly. I do not think he belonged in the infantry. He came and went due to injury or illness. He lasted less than a month before being replaced.

Figure 49 Post August 15, 1969 Replacements Terry Woolums and Cliff Sivadge in mountains near FSB 4-11. Photo provided by Cliff Sivadge.

Figure 50 Post August 15, 1969 Replacement Don Ayres in mountains near FSB 4-11. Photo provided by Don Ayres.

Figure 51 Post August 15, 1969 Replacements Darrel Woods, Tom Nurkiewicz, John Conte, Jim Gain, Cliff Sivadge in mountains near FSB 4-11. Photo provided by Don Ayres.

Figure 52 Sergeant Ronald Owens at FSB Bronco. Photo provided by Barry Suda.

167

CHAPTER 8

MONSOON AND MOUNTAINS

October was a quiet time for us. Lieutenant Rowland was the platoon leader, replacing the last Lieutenant. He'd been an NCO before receiving a commission to Second Lieutenant. He had dark hair, stood five feet, nine inches tall, and weighed 145 pounds. He was lean and fit; he had good leadership traits, and he didn't complain in front of the platoon. Mike and I thought he would be a good Platoon Leader. But, he appeared desperate to engage with the enemy. Mike and I were not too keen on engaging with the enemy.

Early one afternoon, Lieutenant Rowland and the platoon were operating at the base of the mountains and moved into a valley surrounded by mountains on two sides and the river on the other. The valley had overgrown elephant grass as tall as me. At times it led into open, barren spaces. I walked point, creating a trail as I moved forward, and I spotted movement to our front. It looked like an NVA patrol of four or five soldiers. I stopped and dropped to the ground to conceal myself. Slowly, using the tall elephant grass for concealment, I moved back to the platoon and reported the movement to Lieutenant Rowland. Mike saw me coming back to the command group and moved around the line of platoon members to our location.

Lieutenant Rowland said, "Sergeant Haynie, let's double-time to catch up with the enemy you spotted."

I replied, "Sir, it's likely a trap," and pointed to the surrounding mountains. "Chasing the NVA further into the valley isn't a good idea."

Mike said, "Let's call in air strikes or artillery."

The Lieutenant disagreed and said, "Move forward."

As we turned to walk away, he said, "You two are acting like cowards."

I was ready to reply to the Lieutenant, but Mike interrupted and said, "Glyn, let's go."

I was pissed! I moved forward, but slowly, so as not to walk into an ambush. After 10 minutes, the Lieutenant moved to my position and asked, "Why are we moving so slowly?"

I replied, "There may be an ambush ahead!"

The Lieutenant said, "I will take point."

He moved out at a quick pace, passing by me. This stunned me, so I sat there. In two minutes, Mike came up to my position.

Mike asked, "Why aren't we moving, and where is the Lieutenant?"

I pointed forward and said, "He took off that way."

We heard an explosion, so we moved the platoon toward the explosion, thinking the Lieutenant had hit a booby trap. Approaching his position in an open, barren field we found him standing over what appeared to be an old tunnel entrance. He had thrown a grenade into the hole. Now they knew our position. I'm uncertain here, but I'm pretty sure that Captain Kinney contacted Lieutenant Rowland and had him call in artillery and told him not to pursue the enemy. We left the old tunnel, returning the way we came, moving through the open area into the elephant grass.

THE MOUNTAINS

The Quang Ngai province was in a tropical monsoon region, and the annual average temperature was 84 degrees F. The rainy season was from August to December. So it was hot during the day and cold at night, and it rained for days on end. During the monsoon season, we patrolled the mountains and left the flatlands (rice paddies). To the west of Hill 4-11 was a mountain range that was high, steep, and overgrown with jungle vegetation.

These same mountain ranges hid the NVA and VC. They, too, moved to the mountains during the monsoon season. The climb up was physically difficult, hot, wet, and mentally draining, trying to keep a sharp eye out for the enemy, booby traps, and the difficult terrain. Sometimes there were no trails to follow. The point man had to cut a trail with a machete. While crossing streams, we held our weapons out for the person behind us to help them while crossing. Most streams were becoming deep and fast. Fast-moving water could carry a soldier downstream.

Stopping at night, we set up our defensive positions by placing the M-60 gunner first and then the rest of the squad. Once we accomplished that, we moved to the front of our positions and set up claymore mines and trip flares. Then we set up the guard roster for the night, a one-hour or two one-hour shifts. Pulling guard duty meant that you sat with a poncho over you, shivering in the rain, tired, wet, and your body aching as you peered through the slit left open to watch for the enemy. Most nights Mike and I made a lean-to with a poncho, and we sought shelter under it for protection against the rain; this offered warmth generated from our body heat. Two weeks went by without a dry day.

Once our defensive positions were set, we tried to dry out our socks or change them, and inspect ourselves for any foot problems, jungle rot, and leeches. One evening I let out a scream (like a little girl). Mike and another squad member ran over to help.

Mike asked, "What's wrong?"

I replied, "I have leeches on my thighs and balls" as I showed Mike the leeches. This scared the hell out of me. Everyone laughed at my discomfort, which I did not think funny.

I asked Mike, "Help me remove them."

Mike replied, "No way—you're on your own."

The only ways to remove them was to pour salt on them or burn them off with a cigarette. Heck, nobody wanted to help because of the leeches' location, so I had to burn them off myself. I lit a cigarette and placed the burning end against the leech. One by one, they fell to the ground. It took a while, but I removed the leeches. Everything in Vietnam was four times the size as in the US; that made it even worse.

One afternoon we came across an NVA base camp. We moved at a slow pace into the clearing ready to give covering fire for anyone who needed it. First squad reported seeing four NVA soldiers by the creek bed. Once the NVA saw we were there, they took off into the jungle before anyone in the squad could open fire on them. The camp had four hooches and outside fire pits. We started a search of the camp and found documents, company rosters, and a map with marked trails, and that was it.

I discovered several tunnel entrances and called Woolums over to where I was standing.

I said, "Woolums, check this tunnel out."

He replied, "Sergeant Haynie, I'm not going into any tunnel!" I couldn't convince anyone in the squad to go in, so I stripped off my gear and grabbed my flashlight.

I looked at the M-60 gunner and said, "Let me use your .45 pistol." He removed his pistol from the holster and handed it to me.

He said, "Good luck, Sergeant Haynie." I nodded "Thanks."

I lowered myself into the tunnel. Once inside, I sat there waiting for my eyes to adjust to the darkness and then turned on the flashlight. The tunnel didn't have support beams. There were only dirt walls and ceiling, giving me enough height to crawl on my knees along the dirt floor with four or five inches to spare. I could stoop over and walk but found that awkward. I was hoping to find a cache of weapons or food, not enemy soldiers. Twenty feet along the tunnel at the first bend I saw an area four feet high and four feet square, a small room, with several meals sitting on top of a small short stand with steam rising off of the food. I turned around and crawled as fast as I could toward the entrance where I entered the tunnel. Once outside the tunnel, I tossed in a concussion grenade. I hoped that it had run the enemy off or killed them and collapsed the tunnel.

The next day, the company moved up the ridgeline to a higher elevation. Third Platoon was the lead platoon, and First Platoon was behind them in single file (one man behind another). The narrow trail had heavy vegetation on each side. We moved at a slow pace. The line of soldiers stopped after we had been moving two hours. After 10 minutes we moved up the trail again. I heard M-16s being fired to our front. At this point the upward movement stopped, so we sat and waited, enjoying the break from climbing. I opened a can of applesauce to eat while we waited. There was more small-arms fire to the front, and I identified one weapon as an AK-47 firing. Then more M-16s firing, and it got quiet. You could tell which weapon was firing by the distinctive sound it made.

There was movement behind me, and I noticed Captain Kinney and his RTO moving up the trail as fast as he could, moving around the stalled line of men. As he passed where I sat, he dropped his rucksack at my feet.

Captain Kinney said, "Sergeant Haynie, carry my rucksack up while I check out the killed NVA."

Not getting up, I replied, "Yes, Sir," as I stared at the captain as he passed by me. The RTO looked at me and shrugged his shoulders as he went past me, following Captain Kinney.

But I was thinking, *What the hell? Carry your own pack. The NVA isn't going anywhere.* I believed this must have been a first for Captain Kinney to see a dead enemy soldier.

I picked up his rucksack and slung it over my left shoulder as the platoon got the word to move forward. We moved up the trail to the dead-NVA location. Captain Kinney was standing not far away with the handset of the radio against his ear. I walked over and dropped his rucksack at his feet. He didn't even acknowledge that I'd carried it. We continued to move up the mountain as the rain fell again.

Several evenings later Captain Kinney called Mike and me over to the command position. Once we got to his position, we found him sitting and eating his dinner meal.

Mike said, "You want to see us, sir?"

Captain Kinney said, "Sit down. I have something to ask of you two." We sat on the ground, facing the Captain.

Captain Kinney said, "I have an opening in the weapons platoon for a platoon sergeant and want one of you to take the job."

This meant that one of us had to go to training to learn how to support, deploy, and fire mortars because infantrymen didn't receive this specialized training. The training was in Chu Lai.

I asked Captain Kinney, "Can we talk about it and give our decision in the morning?"

Captain Kinney said, "Sure—let me know in the morning."

Once back at our squad position, Mike and I talked of the advantages: No more walking point, not being in the field as much, and an opportunity to move up in a leadership role. The biggest disadvantage was we would no longer be together. We decided being together was more important to us. The next morning we told Captain Kinney we were declining his offer and wanted to stay in First Platoon. Fortunately for us Captain Kinney agreed to our request and didn't push the issue.

In mid-October the platoon received two new replacements. The replacements I remember were Peter Zink (See Appendix H) and Willmer Matson. Barry Suda got a rear job, and John Meyer and Jack Lanzer went back home. Platoon strength was still low.

Figure 53 Barry Suda leaves to be a permanent guard on LZ Snoopy. Photo provided by Barry Suda.

CHAPTER 9

AWARD CEREMONY

STAND-DOWN AND LOCKDOWN

The platoon received word the company would leave for a three-day stand-down. We cleared a landing zone and at the scheduled time popped smoke to alert the Chinook pilot of our location. A squad member guided the pilot to the landing zone, and, as soon as the rear door dropped, the platoon moved into the helicopter. Once loaded, the door closed, and it took off, heading to Chu Lai.

Once we landed in Chu Lai, we departed and headed to the container to store our weapons and ammunition. We went to the building where we slept. Mike and I selected the same bunks as last time. Next was a hot shower and clean, dry clothes. I believe I had worn the same uniform for more than thirty days. After we showered and changed, we went to the mess hall for a steak. We were enjoying a lazy afternoon.

On the first evening Mike and I bought a bottle of Jim Beam and drank. We went to the NCO club after we finished the bottle. After being there for an hour with the Rear Echelon Mother Fuckers (REMFs), Mike noticed two guys staring at him and me.

Mike said, "I don't like the way they are looking at us."

I said, "Let's ask them what the problem is." I approached the two soldiers with Mike following me, and an argument began. Neither one of the two were any bigger than Mike and I, but probably weighed more because they had good food to eat and didn't hump.

One soldier said, "You guys think you are special because you are in the Infantry."

I stated, "Hell, yeah, we are special!"

After that statement, a shoving match started, with the REMF shoving me and Mike stepping in and shoving him back. The room exploded into a western saloon fight. Mike and I ducked low and got the hell out of there.

The next morning Captain Kinney had the company together and said someone reported that his soldiers were not behaving as they should, and the company had to stay within the stand-down compound for the rest of the time. Captain Kinney grounded us! Mike and I told no one it was Mike's fault!

After Captain Kinney's talk, the company clerk called for Mike and me to follow him to the company headquarters location. I thought we were in trouble.

The clerk said, "There will be an awards ceremony this afternoon. You two are recipients of an award."

"We will be there," Mike replied.

He continued, "The ceremony is at 1300 hours. You will receive your awards with other company members."

The company formation would be outside the mess hall. He gave each of us a uniform that was new and pressed, and it had our name tag with unit patches and CIB sewn on and with Sergeant stripes pinned on the collars. We knew that Lieutenant Baxter had submitted us for an award but we had no idea how long it took to be approved, and receiving an award on this day surprised us.

Following our noon meal, the company formed up and the first sergeant had the award recipients line up in front of the company. The Americal Division commander, Major General Lloyd Ramsey, was present to give out the awards. Once everyone was in place, Captain Kinney called the company to attention. Captain Kinney saluted General Ramsey. Then they moved along the line to present each soldier the award they earned. Most were Army Commendation Medals and Bronze Stars for meritorious service. Lieutenant Baxter, Mike, and I were the last three to receive an award. As the General approached each of us, we saluted. The General returned the salute and then pinned the medal to our fatigue pocket on the left side. He shook each of our hands and told us "Job well done" and made time to chit-chat with each of us. I do not recall what the General said.

Lieutenant Baxter received a Bronze Star with a V device (Valor) for actions on August 13, 1969. Mike and I received Silver Stars for the actions on August 13, 1969, and Purple Hearts for being wounded on August 15, 1969.

After the ceremony many of our platoon members and other company soldiers came up to congratulate us, which embarrassed me. Hell, they'd been there with us! I don't know if I deserved a medal; I did what anyone else would have done in my boots. To top it off, the written commendation was not completely truthful. Someone added to the commendation that Mike and I took out and captured a .51 caliber machine gun that day, but that wasn't true. A .51 caliber machine gun was later found abandoned but not by us. Who added the statement about the .51 caliber machine gun and why was a mystery. I assume they were trying to help by embellishing the award narrative so it wouldn't be disapproved. However the narrative didn't tell everything Mike and I had done that day. I can say that Mike had killed and held back the enemy; he retrieved the radio under fire; he helped save Frank Brown; and he helped in providing covering fire and getting the dead out. He assisted in repelling more assaults from the enemy. Yes, he deserved a Silver Star without capturing a machine gun.

It was customary to wear the medal as pinned on for the day awarded. I was proud but embarrassed to receive a medal for that day, so I removed my Silver Star and placed it in my pocket right after the ceremony. I felt I was in the wrong place at the wrong time. I acted on my training, fear, instincts—my survival and the platoon's survival—not bravery.

Mike and I headed back to our bunks after Captain Kinney dismissed the company. We sat and talked about the ceremony and our awards. We decided not to dwell on it any more and enjoy our stand-down. Mike and I purchased more Jim Beam and headed to the mess hall. We grabbed a steak, bread, and baked potato, and sat to eat dinner. We washed the meal down with Jim Beam and Coke. I joined in the continuous poker game for a couple hours and won a good sum of money. Later Mike and I listened to the band until the last song, "We Gotta Get out of This Place," played. We headed back to our bunks to get some much-needed sleep.

I got up late the next day. I lounged on my bunk, reading and talking with Mike. We wanted to relax because tomorrow we were flying back to the field. No more partying this stand-down.

DONUT DOLLIES

Alpha Company moved back to firebase Hill 4-11 after stand-down as the company rotated on for security of the Hill. Lieutenant Rowland assigned our bunkers—the same ones we'd built back in July and August. We noticed that improvements had been made to the company command position, mess hall, and the artillery positions since we'd left in August. The helicopter pad looked larger, too.

I was not a happy person, and I am sure it showed. I still couldn't get the events of the earlier months out of my mind. Even today people ask me about Vietnam, and I reply, "I left as an 18-year-old and came home a 35-year old." An old man in a kid's body! Not much to be happy about. I smiled little.

It was Thanksgiving, and the mess hall prepared the Thanksgiving meal for the companies. The companies out in the field patrolling the AO received hot A's of a turkey dinner delivered by the supply Hueys.

Alpha Company enjoyed their meal at the mess hall served by Donut Dollies. The Donut Dollies, USO volunteers (all American females), tried to make things "normal" for two hours. Mike was sick; he thought he had malaria, so I went for Thanksgiving dinner by myself. I offered to bring Mike something back, but Pete Zink said he would bring Mike his meal.

The Donut Dollies flew in an hour before mealtime, surrounded by security and the company officers. They wore light-colored blouses and skirts, similar to a uniform. Cheerful and smiling, they talked to each soldier as they went through the line to be served their meal. As I moved through the line, loading up with the hot cooked food, I moved forward to the dessert part of the meal.

A Donut Dolly looked at me, smiled, and said, "Here is your dessert if you give us a big smile."

"I don't have a fucking thing to smile about. Give me the dessert," I replied.

Not a happy person. Not a happy place. Now, for the record, I regret my reaction and statement to a person who was only trying to make life normal for several hours. Not a happy time. I am sorry! And thanks, Mike, for never criticizing me for making a fool of myself. And to the Donut Dolly, I apologize.

Figure 54 Lieutenant Baxter after the awards ceremony in Chu Lai November 1969. He received a Bronze Star with V device for actions on August 13, 1969. Photo provided by John Baxter.

CHAPTER 10

CAN'T TAKE IT ANYMORE

GOING ON R & R

It was early to mid-December when I left for R & R to Bangkok, Thailand. I jumped on a resupply chopper heading back to Bronco. I was excited to get away. Once there, I checked in with the first sergeant and checked on my flight to Da Nang. I received my orders for R & R. I got cleaned up, changed uniforms, and packed my bags. I spent the night in a company bunker for my flight the next day. Early the next morning, before daybreak, I headed to the airfield to catch the short flight in a C-130 to Da Nang. Once we'd landed in Da Nang, I checked in with the R & R desk and reserved my seat for the flight to Bangkok, which was leaving in less than an hour. I waited with hundreds of other servicemen who were going on R & R.

A Marine NCO announced it was time to board. We got up from our seats and walked toward the airliner parked on the tarmac. We walked up the stairs to the open door and then moved along the aisle to find an empty seat. I noticed an older guy sitting by the window, so

I sat next to him on the aisle seat. I watched as the men moved along the aisle to find a seat and noticed that every branch of service was represented. There were one hundred or more servicemen going to Bangkok, Thailand.

Once everyone had taken a seat and the doors had been secured, the plane taxied along the runway. We felt the wheels leave the ground and the plane ascend upwards. Everyone on board let out a sigh of relief. As the plane leveled off, the pilot announced the next stop Bangkok, Thailand, and the plane erupted in shouts of joy and laughter. I looked along the aisle and saw only smiles. The soldier I sat next to extended his hand.

He said, "Hello—I'm Arnie."

I shook his hand and replied, "Great to meet you. My name is Glyn."

I asked, "Arnie, what unit are you assigned to?"

Arnie replied, "I'm in aviation, a helicopter pilot."

"You guys are the bravest of brave, and thank you," I replied. Arnie didn't reply, but he smiled, looking embarrassed and uncomfortable after my comment.

Arnie stood five feet, nine inches and weighed 150 pounds, with blond hair, blue eyes, and a round face. We talked most of the flight and became comfortable with each other despite the differences in our ages and ranks; he was 22, and an officer, Warrant Officer 2. Arnie and I spent our R & R together.

Once we landed and departed the plane, we moved into an open room in the terminal and went through a briefing. The airman NCO conducting the briefing appeared bored. In a monotone voice, he told us not to do drugs and covered Thai traditions and Thai culture, too. I think none of us were listening; we wanted to start our R & R. After the briefing, we took military buses to the hotel. Arnie and I went to the Nations Hotel.

The bus stopped at the hotel; 10 of us got off the bus and walked into the hotel lobby carrying our bags. The lobby appeared old but clean. There were two old sofas and four stuffed chairs in the center of the lobby. Right off the lobby was a café that served American food and drinks. The check-in counter, marred with scratches, had a cheerful host on the other side, and he greeted us. The lobby looked comfortable to us. It was a huge step up in luxury from the jungles I'd become accustomed to.

Arnie and I checked in and got our room keys. We agreed to shower and change to civilian clothes and meet in the lobby in 30 minutes. I entered the room and found a neatly made queen-size bed and two nightstands, each holding a small lamp. To the front wall was a large window, covered with worn, thin curtains, with a view of the parking lot and the main street running parallel to the hotel. Under the window sat an old, worn, overstuffed chair. The bathroom had a sink, toilet, and bathtub with a shower. The room was clean but had unfamiliar smells. I undressed and took a quick shower. I hung up my uniform and changed to civilian clothes—a blue polo shirt, khaki slacks, and penny loafers. Arnie and I both arrived on time in the lobby. It was 1000 hours, and we were unsure of what was open this early.

As we discussed our options, a Thai man, 30 years old, wearing black slacks with a white traditional shirt, and dress shoes, approached us and asked, "Do you want a driver for the week?" He told us he was available 24/7 while we were in Bangkok and the cost was $50.00 for the week for both of us.

We both said, "Yes." The driver introduced himself as "George."

George asked, "Where to first?"

Arnie and I looked at each other. Arnie said, "I want a woman."

I said, "Me, too."

George said, "I know the perfect place."

Of course, he did. We got in his car and headed downtown. I had been fighting a war in the jungles the last eight months, but driving on the roads of Bangkok scared the hell out of me. There appeared to be no traffic laws or rules—every car for itself. Fifteen minutes later, George pulled into a parking lot. He parked the car in front of a nondescript building with a sign that read "Happy Happy Massage Bar." Well, this looked interesting. George jumped out and opened the door for us, and we exited the car and followed him into the club.

The club looked like any other, with a long bar with bottles of liquor on mirrored shelves and twenty tables with four chairs per table. The tables were wooden, and the chairs had red-leather cushions. One wall was covered by heavy red drapes. An older Thai man, dressed in a business suit, approached us, and George introduced him as the owner. He asked if we wanted a drink, and we both ordered a bourbon and Coke. He went behind the bar and made the drinks for us and slid them across the bar top. We paid a dollar each for the drinks. As we sipped on our drinks, I noticed that there were no women to be seen.

I asked George, "Where are the women?"

The owner replied, "You will see soon."

We ordered our second drink, and I was thinking something was wrong because we were still the only people in the bar. As the clock on the wall chimed the eleventh hour, the owner walked over to the far wall covered by the red drapes. He grabbed the long white cord and pulled the drapes back. Behind the drapes was a glass-walled room containing 75 women wearing short skirts and blouse or a dress, and each one wore a number over their left breast. They wore heavy makeup and smiled at us. They were young and good-looking.

The owner said, "Pick a number." Three had always been my lucky number!

Number three was a striking Thai woman. Her name was Judy. I assumed it was easier to have an American name. She stood five feet, two inches, weighed about 110 pounds, and appeared to be about 21 years old. She had long, dark hair that flowed past her shoulders and eyes that sparkled. She wore a tight black mini-skirt and a low-cut red-and-white flowered blouse that showed the cleavage of her breast. The black high heels she wore made her appear taller. Her smile would light up a room, and she smiled often. She spoke excellent English. We had a drink and talked. She made it a point to make me comfortable. It was strange to stare into her eyes, sometimes elsewhere, and to hear her voice and laughter. I'd spent months being around men and living in a primitive environment. Arnie selected number 56. She was eye-catching and dressed nicely, too. They sat at another table having a drink and talking.

I noticed George waving for Arnie and me to come over to the bar. I told Judy I would be right back and joined Arnie as we walked over to where George and the owner were standing.

The owner said, "You can pay by the day or the week if you want the girl you picked."

Arnie asked, "How much?"

"It costs $150 for the week or $25 for 24 hours," replied the owner.

I didn't hesitate and said, "Here is $150," as I handed over the cash.

Arnie replied, "I'll take the daily rate." Arnie reached into his pocket and pulled out a $20 bill and a $5 bill and handed it over to the owner.

The first night, the four of us went to the strip alive, with service-men and their female companions. Clubs lined the street, with lights flashing and loud music. Once inside, it was difficult to move through the crowd. Thai women in go-go outfits danced and wiggled on stage to the music. Three Thai men stared at us and talked loudly, pointing at Judy as we approached their table. I thought for sure a fight would erupt, but Judy ignored them and guided us around so a confrontation was not possible. We found a table, and Judy and I danced (well, I tried) and drank the evening away. Arnie and his companion left early to go back to the hotel. This became our nightly ritual.

Back at the hotel, Judy cleaned and bandaged the jungle rot on my arms and legs after she bathed me. She was kind and understanding. I had time to think of my future in Vietnam. I'd often wondered if I would live to my 20th birthday. Those days in May, June, July, and August still haunted me.

I spent seven great days in Bangkok and got to stay in a hotel with running hot water and a bed with a mattress, real food, and ice-cold beverages. Judy took me to tourist sites, the Gold Buddha and temple, the beach, Thai theater, street markets, and the local establishments. I had female companionship, and she was a wonderful guide.

The days and nights flew by, and it was time to return from Bangkok. Arnie and I said our goodbyes to our female companions, and George took us to the airport. Arriving at the airport, George opened the door, and we exited and said our goodbyes to him. We went back through the airport screening and on to our departure gate. In a short time we boarded the plane and departed Bangkok. There were no shouts of joy as the plane left the ground. The flight back was quiet.

LEAVING THE PLATOON

We landed in Da Nang, and the airplane taxied up to a large hangar—the same one where we'd waited for our flight to leave Vietnam. Once the doors opened, we stood to leave the airplane. Arnie and I talked and laughed about our stay in Bangkok as we moved along the aisle toward the door. I was in a good mood!

As soon as I stepped out of the plane onto the steps, the Vietnam smells, heat, and landscape at once made me aware that danger was everywhere; my senses went into high alert, with every muscle tense. This feeling was with you every day, every hour, every minute, and every second in the field. It was exhausting. I made a decision at this point. I said my goodbyes to Arnie, and I jumped on a C-130 going to Chu Lai instead of Duc Pho, where FSB Bronco was located.

Once we landed in Chu Lai, I hitched a ride to the Combat Center where I'd worked before going to First Platoon. The Combat Center had not changed in the last eight months; everything looked the same as the day I left. The company commander who'd commanded the detachment during my first assignment was still the commander. I entered his office and asked the clerk if I could talk to him. The clerk had me wait.

After five minutes, the commander leaned out his office door and said, "Come on in, Sergeant Haynie."

I entered his office and saluted the company commander; he returned my salute. We shook hands, and he asked me to have a seat. We did the normal chit-chat about the last eight months.

Eventually, I asked, "Do you have a job for me?"

He said, "The shipping NCOIC left two days ago, and I need to fill the position."

He continued, "The position holds the formations each morning, checks that everyone is present, and sends the new soldiers to their units for their first assignments in-country. Do you want the job?"

"Yes, Sir," I replied. The company commander got me orders that day.

I returned to FSD Bronco to get my gear and sign out of the company. The First Sergeant wasn't happy. He did not believe my orders and made several phone calls and found that my orders were official. I cleared the company, turning in my field gear and retrieving my medical and personnel records. Then I went back to the orderly room to sign out. The First Sergeant, still angry, let me know in no uncertain terms what he thought of my decision. I got my gear from supply and headed back to the airfield. I left the unit and headed back to Chu Lai with no intentions of returning.

I felt terrible because I'd never discussed this with Mike before I decided, and I did not say goodbye to Mike. I did not say goodbye to anyone. This was something I had to do. Later, I had Mike, Mississippi, Bill Davenport, Alabama, and other platoon members visit. My hooch was their home, too. We sat on the front steps of my hooch and drank Jim Beam and watched the ocean and talked. A couple weeks later, Mike got a rear job in supply at the company headquarters at Duc Pho. I felt better knowing Mike was out of the field.

I had been in Chu Lai for six or seven days, and it was Christmas Eve. The Bob Hope Christmas Tour was in Chu Lai, and I had the afternoon to myself. I hitched a ride with the company jeep and headed to the show location. Arriving an hour early, I found the place packed with thousands of soldiers. I found myself a good distance from the stage. But I had a great time watching Bob Hope and Connie Stevens. Mr. Hope, funny as ever, played up to the audience of soldiers.

I remember that Connie Stevens sang the song "Wedding Bell Blues" and had several soldiers on stage with her as she sang and teased with them. After she finished singing, she asked each soldier their name, and each responded, "Bill." But the last soldier responded, "John," and that got a good laugh. I always assumed they selected the soldiers because of their name being "Bill."

CHAPTER 11

WHEN DOES IT STOP?

I was learning my new job and found it easy. I coordinated with the units by telephone and attempted to make sure they received the replacements they required for their Military Occupation Skill (MOS) and rank. Each morning I held a formation on the dirt road in front of the shipping shed and had a roll call. Soldiers shipped to their units every day of the week, Sunday through Saturday. Every one who shipped to their unit that day moved into the shed. The shed was a large one-room building filled with benches and had a dirt floor. The upper half of the walls had window screen attached to the length of each wall to allow the air to circulate. The rest I dismissed or assigned them to a detail. I stayed at the shed with the replacements until their unit arrived to get them. I told soldiers going to my old company about the people they could count on and trust. Once they got to the field, they should seek them out. I told them to seek Mike Dankert at supply and that he would help them out. The shipping shed was near the beach. A cooler breeze came inland, which made it more enjoyable while waiting for the replacements to be picked up by their units.

During this early period at the Combat Center, I got sick. I woke up with a fever, chills, and body aches and could hardly stay awake during the day. Then, the next day, I felt good. This went on for a week, and my NCOIC told me to go on sick call because it sounded as if I had malaria. On sick call I saw a medic, and he requested a doctor test me. They tested for malaria but it came back negative. The diagnosis was probably "jungle fever." I'm still not sure what "jungle fever" meant. I took another week to recover. The commander and NCOIC weren't pleased that I had to miss work.

LEARNING OF JANUARY 14

On January 14, 1970, Alpha Company and the First Platoon engaged in a firefight with the enemy and suffered casualties. Killed were Gary Morris and Roger Kidwell. Wounded were Bill Davenport and Pete Zink; they were medevacked to the Chu Lai hospital.

Mike called me and told me what had happened. He said he was flying to Chu Lai that afternoon and asked if I would pick him up at the airfield to check on Bill and Pete at the hospital. From our conversation, I learned that the enemy had killed Morris and Kidwell. I knew Gary Morris well but did not know Roger Kidwell. It saddened me to hear the enemy had killed or wounded more platoon members. I thought I'd escaped from death and misery.

I had the company jeep and was waiting for Mike at the airfield. Mike arrived by C-130. We hugged, said hello, and headed to the hospital. We checked on Bill first, and he had a wound in the leg. His wound would heal fast, and he didn't need to go to Japan. We found him in good spirits, and he did his best to display that big, wide smile of his. I told him once the hospital released him, I would do what I could to get him a rear job with me. This perked him up, and his smile came back.

We visited Pete next. The first thing I noticed was how swollen and cut-up his face was. This shocked me. I barely recognized him, and I hoped my expression didn't alarm him. If my expression of alarm was showing, he didn't let on. Pete had a bandage on his left hand to cover shrapnel wounds. He was in good spirits and assured us he was fine, would heal fast, and go home soon. Pete always had a positive attitude. Not long after our visit, the hospital transferred Pete to Japan or the States—I'm not sure which one.

WHAT HAPPENED JANUARY 14, 1970,
AS TOLD BY CLIFF SIVADGE

Alpha Company had a combat assault into the foothills, three klicks from Hill 4-11. Due to the rough terrain, the choppers couldn't drop each platoon within the same logistical landing zone. As a result, the company separated as a unit. The area contained tall grass which we later used for cover but not protection.

After First Platoon had begun reconnaissance of the area, members of second squad observed two enemy soldiers in the distance, sitting and smoking on a large rock. The enemy soldiers were unaware or our presence. They relayed this information to our platoon leader who decided second squad needed to seek cover and, once in position, engage the enemy with small weapons. Our squad attempted to gain strategic positions and our M-60 machine gunner gave support for those carrying M-16s.

Within minutes, the platoon leader gave the order to engage the enemy with M-16s. Second squad soon discovered that our surprise attack had awakened a sleeping dog and within less than thirty minutes, what we hoped a short firefight became a full-blown battle. The NVA soldiers, we soon learned, had chi-com grenades and RPGs.

Our enemy, who we later learned were NVA forces, ordered snipers to circle around and flank second squad to the left and right of our positions. It was customary for the French who fought the Vietnamese for nine years before U.S. occupation, to build walls three to four feet high constructed of small circular stones. These stone walls provided excellent protection for the NVA snipers and they had second squad pinned down, our only escape route being back up the hill to our rear.

My position during this firefight was beside Lieutenant Litneger, our platoon leader. I recall hearing a loud explosion behind us and to our left. I crawled back up the hill to check out what had happened and discovered that Zink, a member of second squad, wounded by shrapnel from what I assumed was a chi-com grenade. Zink suffered injuries to his face, primarily to his eye, but Zink spoke and it appeared he suffered no other major wounds.

I low-crawled along the hill to join my platoon leader and I'm not sure how much time elapsed before we heard another explosion further out and to the right of our position.

A horrific scream from a squad member followed the explosion. The following day we learned what had transpired. The squad member's name was Gary Morris. He had taken a direct hit from an RPG and killed instantly. Gary had advanced too near the enemy's position, allowing them to fire the fatal shot from their vantage point. Unknown at the time the enemy killed Roger Kendall and wounded Bill Davenport during the same exchange.

During the firefight, the platoon leader radioed Hill 4-11 requesting whatever air support might be available. Our squad's position was too close in proximity to the enemy to expect much, but we were in hopes we might get a Huey with two M-60 machine gunners to fire and allow our squad to retreat up the hill to a safer position. Unfortunately, the only chopper dispatched was a "Loach" which, although not equipped with M-60 machine gunners, proved to be helpful. I heard the chopper making its approach as it maneuvered to Lieutenant Litneger's and my position. It's difficult to convey the pride I felt for this heroic chopper pilot as he hovered over our enemy's position, diverting their attention and gunfire away from our squad. The chopper pilot communicated he observed what he believed was at least twelve dead enemy soldiers. He was taking fire from the enemy and within a short time forced to return to Hill 4-11. We later learned that the Loach chopper received thirteen bullet hits.

Another platoon from Alpha Company arrived and provided added support, allowing second squad to withdraw back up the hill to safety. The firefight lasted long enough that darkness soon fell upon the company and as a result, trip flares couldn't be set out. Guard duty that night was scary for everyone, knowing what had taken place that day. I remember a phrase an instructor taught me at the combat center of pulling nightly guard duty in the bush. The instructor said "When you're alone at your guard position, staring into the blackness, wondering if you heard something or not, your asshole tightened up so you couldn't pound a ten-penny nail in it with a fifteen pound sledge." Much to the relief of everyone who pulled guard duty the night passed without incident.

On the morning of January 15, we revisited the site of the earlier day's firefight to extract our casualties. As we approached, the position where second squad first engaged the enemy, we noticed that not one of the enemy soldiers' bodies was visible. During the night, the NVA had removed their dead (as most combat veterans are aware, Vietnamese believe in reincarnation, but only if their bodies are recovered by their own people). We learned later that day how our enemy did this.

I had volunteered to help remove Gary Morris. As its common for the NVA to booby trap the bodies of their enemy with grenades, as a precaution, we tied claymore wire to Gary's body to roll him over, but the claymore wire proved too weak. We gave up on avoiding any danger from booby traps and placed Gary in a body bag. With the help of several second squad members, we lifted Gary into the dust-off chopper that was hovering nearby. Later another platoon member told me they put Roger on the same dust-off.

We then began a recon of the entire battle field, focusing on the locations of our enemy from the earlier day's firefight. Although our company had passed this location at least once during the earlier six months, we soon learned that our enemy had been surveying Hill 4-11 from this vantage point for a time. The enemy position had huge boulders that formed a natural labyrinth of cracks and crevices between the various rock formations. After further investigation of these large openings between the boulders, we discovered a natural pathway which led to an underground tunnel. This tunnel allowed our enemy to remove their casualties from the night before the firefight.

The squad leader asked for volunteers to enter and survey the discovered tunnel. While I do not recall the name of the soldier who agreed to this assignment, I applaud his bravery. The life expectancy of Tunnel Rats was, as most Viet Nam vets are aware, short. The NVA had evacuated the tunnel; but, the enemy abandoned the articles in their haste to leave. Items discovered in the tunnel included: bloodied rags (from wounds suffered by our enemy the previous day) and five-gallon sealed aluminum containers filled with fish heads soaking in oil. We discovered no weapons or ammunition in the tunnel. I wasn't privileged to information of the disposition or destruction of the tunnel discovered on January 15, 1970 by Alpha Company. The commanding officers of Alpha Company coordinated efforts with military intelligence teams that led to the tunnel's destruction.

Mike visited me several times, and we talked on the phone after he got his rear job. On his visits Mike and I sat out front and had several of our favorite drinks, bourbon and Coke, and talked about First Platoon. Mike's visits reminded me how much I missed him.

PRISONER TRANSPORT

Early one morning my NCOIC notified me I was to transport a prisoner to Long Binh Jail (LBJ) near Saigon by C-130 and turn him over to the military police there. This wasn't an unusual order—just an extra duty assignment. The military police would meet us at the airfield. I asked my NCOIC for and received permission for Mike to go with me. This coincided with one of Mike's visits. I told Mike I'd gotten permission for him to go with me. Mike said, "Let's go."

We went to the arms room, and each of us checked out a .45 caliber pistol and two clips of ammunition. After strapping on the .45s, we got a jeep and driver and drove to the Division military police stockade to pick up the prisoner. After we signed for him and got the handcuff key, we put him in the back seat of the jeep with Mike and I sat in the passenger seat up front. The driver headed to the airfield for our flight.

The prisoner, an American soldier, was constantly running his mouth, complaining about everything and everybody in or out of uniform. He went on and on ranting and waving his handcuffed hands. We seldom understood exactly what he was complaining about. Mike told him to shut up and sit still. We'd heard enough. Finally, there was silence. He was getting to Mike more than me. We parked the jeep, escorted him into the plane, and sat him in a seat between Mike and me. The plane taxied and lifted off the runway. Once in the air, he started ranting and raving again about the Army and "the world." How the Army had screwed everything up and he wouldn't take it any longer. Finally, Mike reached his breaking point and told him, "Listen, you asshole—I'm short, and I don't need this shit. Shut your mouth while we're on the plane or I will shoot your sorry ass, and nobody will care." He remained quiet so it must have worked.

We landed, and there were two MPs who met us and signed for the prisoner. Mike and I got on the next flight back to Chu Lai. The driver met us and drove us back to the Combat Center. We turned in our weapons to the arms room. And once we returned to my hooch, we opened the Jim Beam and sat on the front porch talking, drinking, and enjoying the sunset.

Several days after Mike left, John DeLoach (Mississippi) came by for a two-day visit. John looked well, but I could tell he was mentally and physically tired. John told me he was going to the Artillery. He would be out of the field. I told John he'd made a good decision. Being at a fire support base was safer than humping in the field.

John and I spent the time after I got off work having a good dinner at the mess hall, playing cards, and relaxing on the front porch, watching the South China Sea and the sunset. One evening we went to the outdoor theater to catch a movie, I cannot remember the movie. John left on the third morning, and I wouldn't see him again until forty-six years later.

After Bill Davenport got released from the hospital, I asked the company commander to have Bill replace me as the Shipping NCOIC; he agreed. Bill and I had several weeks of overlap before I left. It was great to have Bill around, and it made me feel less guilty for my decision to leave the field and the platoon. We had many talks about our time together with First Platoon while enjoying the view of the South China Sea and sipping on our Jim Beam. After I left to go home, I didn't see him again until 1986, in Portland, Oregon. Mike, Chuck Council, and I got together for a small reunion. Bill appeared the same, but he'd lost that large smile he'd always had. I believe our Vietnam days still haunted him. Time does not always heal.

Figure 55 Bill Davenport at Chu Lai Hospital recovering from a leg wound received January 14, 1970. Photo provided by Glyn Haynie.

Figure 56 Pete Zink at Chu Lai hospital WIA January 14, 1970. Photo provided by Glyn Haynie.

Figure 57 Glyn Haynie at Combat Center February 1970 (note jungle rot scars on arm). Photo provided by Glyn Haynie.

Figure 58 Bill Davenport at Americal Combat Center February 1970. Bill still had his smile after being wounded January 14, 1970. Photo provided by Glyn Haynie.

Figure 59 Mike Dankert at rear job in FSB Bronco February 1970. Photo provided by Mike Dankert.

CHAPTER 12

GOING HOME

The Army scheduled me to leave Vietnam March 10, 1970, but I received a three-day drop and was rescheduled to leave March 7, 1970. I called Mike to let him know that I was leaving early and to ask if he could come up to Chu Lai. Mike got permission and arrived on March 6. We had dinner together at the mess hall and then went back to my hooch and sat on the front porch and drank Jim Beam, reflecting on our time together. We never talked about the combat actions, only the fun times like stand-down, R & R, the platoon members, and the funny or strange circumstances we had together. It wasn't awkward to say goodbye to Mike, but it felt like I was deserting him.

The next morning my ride pulled up to the hooch. We hugged, and I jumped into the jeep, heading to the Chu Lai airfield to start my journey home. You'd think I would be extremely happy, but I felt sad that Mike and I might not see each other again.

I flew from Chu Lai to Cam Ranh Bay for the long flight to Fort Lewis, Washington. Once we landed at Cam Ranh Bay, we walked out the back ramp of the C-130 and followed a sergeant to a building for final out-processing. They searched our gear and verified our orders for the flight home. It surprised me at the number of weapons, grenades, and even explosives that the MPs found while searching our bags. They gave us a last opportunity to exchange any MPC we had to dollars. If you got to the States with MPC, it was worthless.

As we waited for word to board the plane, a plane landed, and FNGs in brand-new jungle fatigues departed the plane. They walked right past our location and stared at the veterans waiting to return home. Several veterans made disparaging remarks to the FNGs, but I was quiet and felt sorry for them.

I looked around at the returning veterans. Seeing a familiar face, I yelled out, "Michael Smith," and he looked up and saw me. With a big smile, he yelled back, "Hello, Haynie." We'd gone through airborne school together and had flown to Vietnam together. He got assigned to the Americal Division the 196th Infantry Brigade. We had not seen each other for 12 months. I maneuvered through the throng of soldiers until I reached him, and we shook hands and then embraced. We were both glad to be going home. He had those sad, piercing eyes of a veteran behind his large smile.

The sergeant instructed us to follow him back out to the tarmac to the waiting airliner. We walked up the steps to enter the cabin of the plane and moved along the aisle to find a seat. Smith and I found two empty seats next to each other and sat for the long flight home. Once the plane had taxied along the runway and left the ground, everyone was still quiet, but, after the pilot announced that we were at a safe altitude and that we could remove our seat belts, the plane erupted with shouts of joy. Vietnam was behind us! Smith and I occupied our time catching up on what we had been doing this last year while sipping on a few bourbons and Cokes. We played poker—which he was winning. But before we landed, I believe he allowed me to win my money back. Eventually we got a short nap. We flew to Japan and then Alaska and landed at Fort Lewis.

We went through the processing and received new Class A dress uniforms for the flight back home. My duty assignment was Fort Benning, Georgia, my hometown. Smith was getting out of the Army and going home to Boston, Massachusetts. The detachment NCOIC told us the mess hall had a steak dinner for us, so we went to the mess hall to have a good meal before the flight home. While we ate our steak dinner, supply tailored our uniform and sewed on our rank. We had our own awards and decorations to pin on our uniform. The Army repaid you for any hardship by providing a steak dinner. We appreciated the steak.

Shortly after the meal, 50 of us loaded onto a bus wearing our dress uniforms, with the award ribbons and badges pinned to the correct location and our rank sewn onto the sleeves. The bus pulled into the Seattle, Washington, terminal, and we unloaded carrying our duffle bags on our shoulders. Smith and I checked in with the airlines, left our baggage, and received our tickets. We had two hours before our flight, so we headed to the bar. We sat at a table with two other guys who'd been on our flight home from Vietnam and talked about what we would do after we got home.

The waitress came to our table to take our drink order, and I ordered last. I said, "A bourbon and Coke, please." She asked for my identification card, which I gave her, thinking being military might allow me to buy a drink. But she said I couldn't be served because I was only nineteen. I got pissed, but I expected that this would happen. Smith said he wanted to change his order and ordered two bourbons, and the waitress left and returned with the drinks. She set both drinks Michael ordered in front of him, and he looked her in the eye and slid one of the drinks toward me. How ironic! I was not old enough to vote either, but old enough to carry a weapon, fight a war, and kill so that others could vote and drink alcohol.

I told Smith thanks for the drink. While we talked, I heard the announcement that my flight was ready to board. We exchanged our parents' home phone numbers, hugged, and said goodbye. As I walked toward my gate, I noticed people staring at me, and several families and individuals even moved to the other side of the walkway as I approached. Maybe it was me and my imagination I wasn't sure. I boarded, and the flight departed, heading toward Atlanta, Georgia.

The flight was uneventful, and, once we landed, I moved along the aisle to the front cabin door to exit. I followed the passengers into the waiting section, where my mother and father were waiting to greet me. I hugged my mother and then shook my father's hand. As we shook hands, I sensed he was proud of me, but he never said so. On the ride home, outside Atlanta, my dad asked if I was hungry, and I said, "Yes—a hamburger, fries, and a chocolate milkshake." He stopped, and I ordered my meal and ate it on the drive home; the meal tasted better than I remembered from a year earlier. The hour-long ride to Columbus went fast as we talked about Columbus, the Army, and my old friends. Arriving home, there were no bands, no parade, no one to welcome me home but my parents and my sister. Wayne was in Korea and would not be home until early December.

The first night home, I showered and put on my civilian clothes and started to walk out the front door to go to the Krystal's (White Castle if you are from another region.) where my friends had hung out during high school.

My mother stopped me and asked, "Where are you going?"

I replied, "Out."

She continued, "You need to be home by eleven." This was my curfew while I was in high school.

She asked again, "Where are you going?"

I angrily replied, "To find an apartment!"

I was hoping for a big welcome home from my friends, but after I arrived, most said, "Hey, Haynie! Where have you been? Haven't seen you in a while."

The End

AFTERWORD

In the military, it's said that men create a bond from combat, and this bond is understood only inside the military. First Platoon was my family during my year in Vietnam and every day after I returned. We are all brothers and have a bond that cannot be explained. We fought, bled, cried, played, and partied together. After the enemy killed or wounded one of us, the pain we felt was unimaginable. As men, we unapologetically held another platoon member during their grief. I still miss the platoon members who never came back home. I regret I didn't get to know them better.

The platoon members helped each other without any questions. We would give our life to save another. We helped carry each other's load and share our rations, water, ammunition, and packages from home without hesitation. First Platoon members are my brothers, and the bond we formed in combat will always exist.

Mike Dankert and I formed a special bond of brotherhood. We pulled guard duty together, even though it was an individual task, allowing one to nap while the other was vigilant. We shared the same wet ground, the shallow foxhole, our rations, the unsweetened Kool-Aid, the same fears and horrors of combat. Mike didn't choose Vietnam or the Army.

But he accepted it. He became an outstanding soldier and leader. We had complete trust in the other, even with our lives at stake. It was as if Mike and I had come together to protect each other from harm. The names "Dankert" and "Haynie" became one. You would not find one without the other. I respect Mike and look up to him as a soldier, my best friend, and, yes, a brother.

REMEMBERING THE FALLEN

- ★ Bruce Tufts
- ★ Juan Ramos
- ★ Eldon Reynolds
- ★ Robert Swindle
- ★ Jerry Ofstedahl
- ★ Richard "Rebel" Wellman
- ★ Joseph Mitchell
- ★ Paul Ponce
- ★ Daniel Carey
- ★ James Anderson
- ★ Roger Kidwell
- ★ Gary Morris
- ★ Willmer Matson

POSTSCRIPT: THE REUNION

Through the years I thought of my platoon brothers and wondered where they were and how they were doing. I was getting older, and I didn't want to forget them or the brothers who didn't come home. In April 2015, I created a small website listing all the platoon members I could remember. I'd stayed in contact with Mike Dankert, Dusty Rhoades, and Chuck Council through the years and asked for their help to add names and dates. The platoon website grew from that day. Now I was on a mission.

Then I began to concentrate on finding platoon members. Through hundreds of hours using the computer to research and as many hours making telephone calls, I contacted 26 more platoon members for a total of 30; 8 of the 30 died since returning from Vietnam. Most platoon members I contacted were receptive to being contacted even though they may not have remembered me or I them. Our memory is a strange storage medium! We re-connected in a short time. A few members I found wanted no contact. I did not pressure them. I found that Ray "Alabama" Hamilton and Charlie Deppen had lived a couple hours from me for the last 20 years. Small world!

Sherrie and I took a trip in the summer of 2015 to meet some of the platoon members I'd found and had not seen in 46 years. We scheduled the trip and met each member for lunch or dinner near their home. We met John "Mississippi" DeLoach and daughter Kelli, John Baxter and his wife Carol, Maurice Harrington, and Charlie Deppen and his wife Melanie and daughter Grace. Two weeks later we met Ray "Alabama" Hamilton for lunch. Meeting these platoon members and their families was an awesome experience. Time had no impact on our relationship of 46 years ago. We didn't even talk about Vietnam; we had to catch up on 46 years first.

Mike and I decided to host a reunion for the platoon members we'd found and their spouses. From July 14 through July 17, 2016, we hosted the reunion in Dallas, Texas. It took time and coordination, but we got 13 platoon members and the sister, Gloria, of Juan Ramos (KIA July 14, 1969) to attend. We had 31 people attend the reunion, including platoon members, spouses, four children, and two grandchildren. It was unbelievable to see my platoon brothers sit together and talk as if the 47 years that had gone by did not exist.

I found the spouses remarkable. They met and embraced and talked as if they had known each other the last 47 years and had shared the same experiences. It was amazing!

ATTENDEES

- ★ Mike Dankert
- ★ Dusty and Joanna Rhoades
- ★ Glyn and Sherrie Haynie and son David and wife Tarie
- ★ Chuck and Alice Council
- ★ John DeLoach and Jan Jacobo
- ★ Maurice and Irene Harrington
- ★ Charlie and Melanie Deppen and daughter Grace
- ★ Ray and Chris Hamilton
- ★ Dennis and Peggy Stout

- ★ Don Ayres and son Sean
- ★ Leslie Pressley and Brenda Cartee
- ★ Cliff and Laura Sivadge
- ★ Gloria Ramos (sister of Juan Ramos)
- ★ Fred and Dixie Katz (2 Grandkids)

Figure 60 Photograph taken at Reunion 2016. Sitting, left to right: Gloria Ramos, Maurice Harrington, Mike Dankert, Fred Katz. Standing, left to right: Glyn Haynie, Don Ayres, Cliff Sivadge, Dusty Rhoades, Leslie Pressley, Charlie Deppen, Chuck Council, Dennis Stout, John "Mississippi" DeLoach and Ray "Alabama" Hamilton.

APPENDIX A

FIRST PLATOON MEMBERS (PANEL AND ROW IS THE LOCATION ON THE WALL)

Name	Stat	Date	Panel	Row
Baxter, John				
Wakeling, Victor				
Rowland, Harold				
Pressley, Leslie				
Daron, Terrance				
Meyer, John				
Windows, Michael				
Sailors, Ron				
Swindle, Robert	KIA	13-Aug-69	19W	35
Wellman, Richard	KIA	13-Aug-69	19W	36
Owens, Ronald				
Mitchell, Joseph	KIA	15-Aug-69	19W	46
Ponce, Paul	KIA	15-Aug-69	19W	47
Ramos, Juan	KIA	14-Jul-69	21W	120
Reynolds, Eldon	KIA	14-Jul-69	21W	120

Name	Stat	Date	Panel	Row
Rhoades, Timothy	WIA	14-Jul-69		
Council, Chuck				
Okino, Ryan	WIA	15-Aug-69		
Suda, Barry				
Harrington, Maurice				
Lanzer, Jack				
Smith, Robert				
Stout, Michael				
Stout, Dennis				
McVey, Warren				
Plummer, Michael				
Sanchez, Amby				
Tufts, Robert	KIA	14-Jun-69	22W	50
Ofstedahl, Jerry	KIA	13-Aug-69	19W	33
Carey, Danny	KIA	15-Aug-69	19W	43
Hamilton, Ray	WIA	15-Aug-69		
Dankert, Michael	WIA	14-Jun-69		
		15-Aug-69		
Haynie, Glyn	WIA	15-Aug-69		
Brown, Frank	WIA	13-Aug-69		
Cameron, Donald				
Buff, Allyn				
Anderson, James	KIA	15-Aug-69	19W	43
Davenport, Bill	WIA	15-Aug-69		
		14-Jan-70		
DeLoach, John				
Zink, Pete	WIA	14-Jan-70		
Zwiesler, Jerry				
Thompson, Tommy	WIA	15-Aug-69		
Deppen, Charles	WIA	02-Jul-69		
		15-Aug-69		

Name	Stat	Date	Panel	Row
Rowe, Dennis	WIA	14-Jun-69		
VanDyke, Nick	WIA	14-Jun-69		
Sivadge, Clifton				
Morris, Gary	KIA	14-Jan-70	14W	34
Kidwell, Roger	KIA	14-Jan-70	14W	33
Jurgensen, Jack				
Woolums, Terry				
Oliver, Archie				
Kingsbury, David				
Conti, John				
Ayres, Donald				
Teaberry, Wilbert				
Strauch, Manuel				
Abernathy, David				
Thornton, James				
Hardman, Michael				
Nurkiewicz, Tom				
Katz, Fred				
Matson, Willmer	KIA	15-Mar-70	13W	151

KIA—Killed in Action

WIA—Wounded in Action

Members added from memory.

APPENDIX B

OBITUARY FOR MICHAEL WINDOWS PUBLISHED BY AKERS FUNERAL HOME

Michael H. Windows, 65, of Adelphia Road, Everett, passed away on Sunday, October 5, 2014 at home. He was born on February 22, 1949 in Pittsburgh, PA; a son of the late Hubert and Mildred (Brady) Windows. On February 30, 1997 in Cumberland, Maryland; he married Connie L. (Strait) Windows. She preceded him in death on March 6, 2013.

He is survived by a step-son: David L. Strait and wife Tammy (Price), Everett, PA Step-Grandchildren: Megan, Tyler, Trevor and Madison Strait; Sister-in-law: Linda Windows;

Three Nieces and Two Nephews.

He was preceded in death by two brothers and a sister-in-law: Kenneth Windows and Jack Windows and wife Mary Ann.

Mike attended Seven Dolors of the B.V.M. Catholic Church, Beans Cove. He attended Bedford High School. He served in the United States Army during the Vietnam War.

Mike was a jack of all trades working various places throughout the years, but mainly working in the metal industry. He was a member of the Everett Redman Social Club and the Everett American Legion Post No. 08. He enjoyed hunting.

Family and Friends may call at the Akers Funeral Home, 299 Raystown Road, Everett on Thursday, October 9, 2014 from 1:00 PM until the hour of service.

Memorial Service will be held in the Chapel at Akers Funeral Home on Thursday, October 9, 2014 at 2:00 PM with Father Derek Fairman officiating. Everett Area Honor Guard will be conducting military rites. Burial will be held privately at Seven Dolors of the B.V.M. Catholic Church Cemetery, Beans Cove.

APPENDIX C

OBITUARY FOR MICHAEL STOUT
PUBLISHED BY THE HAWK EYE

Michael L. Stout, 37, of rural West Burlington, died from complications of cancer Thursday, December 18.

He was born January 25, 1949, in Burlington, the son of LeRoy and Lois Brockway Stout. On October 18, 1975, in Hamilton, Illinois, he married Lori Humphry.

Mr. Stout was a fireman paramedic at the Iowa Army Ammunition Plant. He was a veteran of the Vietnam War, receiving the Purple Heart and Bronze Star. He was a member of the Pastores Class, a member of the board of directors of Beacon House, a volunteer fireman in West Burlington, a member of the West Burlington Lions and belonged to Grace United Methodist Church.

Surviving are his wife; two sons, Wesley and Travis; one brother, Dennis Stout of New London; his father and stepmother, Mr. and Mrs. LeRoy Stout of Bettendorf; and his mother and stepfather, Mr. and Mrs. Robert Bratton of New London. Visitation will be 7 and 8 PM Friday at the Sheagren Funeral Home.

Funeral services will be at the Grace United Methodist Church at 2 PM Saturday with the Reverend David Streyfeller officiating. Burial will be in Aspen Grove Cemetery, will military rites at the grave. A memorial has been established at Sheagren Funeral Home.

APPENDIX D

OBITUARY FOR BILL DAVENPORT PUBLISHED BY THE
DAILY NEWS ONLINE

Longtime local resident William Davenport, 62, of Longview passed away July 30, 2011, at the Veteran's Administration Rehabilitation Center in Vancouver.

He was born Dec. 13, 1948, in Yakima, and moved to the local area 51 years ago.

Bill served in the Army during the Vietnam War from 1969 to 1970. He was awarded the Bronze Star with an oak leaf, a Purple Heart with two oak leaves and a Combat Infantry Badge. Bill was an emergency medical technician with American Medical before retiring in 2006. He enjoyed fishing with his buddies at county line.

He is survived by a sister, Linda Davenport of Long Beach; a brother and sister-in-law, Ben and Nancy Davenport of Castle Rock; two nephews, Benjamin Davenport of Chehalis and Ryan Davenport of Castle Rock; a niece, Lindsey Lonner of Kelso; two great-nephews, Chase and Nathan; and two great-nieces, Kehna and Maddison. Bill was preceded in death by a brother, Bob Davenport.

Inurnment with full military honors was at the Willamette National Cemetery in Portland. Cremation has taken place under the direction of Davies Cremation & Burial Service, Vancouver.

APPENDIX E

I transcribed the information below from the news article.

VC SERENADE WASTED ON INFANTRY BY SP4 TONY SWINDELL, *SOUTHERN CROSS NEWSPAPER*

LZ-4-11 – It was a clear, peaceful night for the 11th Bde's A Co., 3rd Bn., 1st Inf. on their new firebase until the Viet Cong decided to hold an impromptu concert for the Americal Division soldiers.

"It was about 9 or 10 PM when I began hearing the song 'Where Have All the Flowers Gone?'" explained 1LT Lewis D. Adams Jr. (West Point, Ga.), artillery forward observer for A Co. "Then this voice came on, asking us why we were fighting in Vietnam. It was really strange because the voice was very clear and spoke in excellent English."

SP4 James Shelton (Raytown, Mo.), radio telephone operator for the company commander, continued the story. "The first song was 'Where Have All the Flowers Gone,' followed by 'Oh Suzanna' and 'North to Alaska.' As far as I could tell the songs were original American versions.

"Then this guy started telling us to come over to his side and help get rid of the 'trouble-makers' in Vietnam. He added that this was a special broadcast for all soldiers, officers and ARVN's. They must have thought we had interpreters up on the hill because part of the time they spoke in Vietnamese."

While the company listened in wonderment to the music and broadcast, 1LT Adams called for artillery to silence the talkative Communist PSYOP team which he estimated 800 to 900 meters northwest of the firebase.

"I must have directed over 100 rounds into the area," commented 1LT Adams, "and I was sure that we must have either gotten them or at least scared them away. But as soon as the noise subsided and the smoke cleared away they were broadcasting again chiding us for our poor marksmanship. They said if we didn't leave Vietnam we would be wiped out like we were in Korea. It was really something."

SP4 Shelton, who was listening closely to the broadcast and relaying what he heard to the battalion tactical operations center at LZ Bronco, added: "Whatever broadcasting system they were using was big to cover that distance so clearly. We think it was a portable PA outfit with a remote microphone so the VC could broadcast in a bunker or under cover safe from the artillery."

After about 15 minutes, the Vietnam-style disc jockey and propagandist ended his message apparently unharmed, but he would have been disappointed at the reaction from the amused soldiers. Several commented that the broadcast was "better than a show." (11th IO)

APPENDIX F

OBITUARY FOR ALLYN BUFF PUBLISHED BY THE WESTERN NEWS

Allyn Paul Buff, 64, of Libby died Wednesday, July 24, 2013, at his home. He was born Dec. 13, 1948, in Pomona, Calif. He attended school and lived most of his young life in Cucamonga, Calif.

Allyn was drafted into the U.S. Army in 1969 and served his country in Vietnam, earning two Bronze Service Stars as a combat infantryman. He was honorably discharged from service in 1971.

Upon returning home Allyn married his sweetheart, Darrylyn Stockrahm, in 1972. They had three children. Their family moved to Libby in 1979. The couple divorced in 1984 but remained friends until Darrylyn's death.

Allyn spent his early years in Libby working as a mechanic at Libby Dam until 1990. He then purchased a well-drilling rig and started his little company, Clearwater Drilling, with the help of his dear friend, Marlene Raitt.

When he wasn't drilling holes in the ground all over Lincoln County, the avid fisherman could be found somewhere on his beloved Kootenai

River trying to best his own personal record catch of a 19-pound, 34-inch rainbow trout. Many people also knew him as a classic-car and hot-rod enthusiast and he spent much of his time tinkering with his old Chevys.

Allyn was preceded in death by his mother, Alice Rantos. He is survived by his daughters, Cyndi (Joe) Miller of Libby, Paula Buff of Seattle and Lynda Buff of Libby; his sister, Lynn (D.J.) Martin of Arizona; brothers, Rick (Gloria) Tham of Prescott, Ariz., Chris (Sherri) Tham of Petaluma, Calif.; an uncle, Paul Buff of Mobile, Ala.; four granddaughters, Natesha, Tiahna, Shalen and Dustina; and numerous nieces, nephews, good friends and neighbors.

A funeral service will be held at the Libby Cemetery at 3 PM Saturday, Aug. 10, with military honors. Arrangements are by Schnackenberg & Nelson Funeral Home & Crematory in Libby.

APPENDIX G

OBITUARY FOR TERRY WOOLUMS PUBLISHED BY GRACELAND / FAIRLAWN FUNERAL HOME

Terry L. Woolums, 63 formerly of Decatur passed away on Sunday, January 20, 2013 in Danville. Terry was born March 30, 1949 in Decatur, IL, the son of Arthur and Mollie (Seay) Woolums. He graduated from Mt. Zion high school and proudly served his country in Viet Nam as a member of 3rd Battalion, 1st Infantry Regiment.

Terry is survived by his daughter Mollie Woolums of Indianapolis, grandchildren, Tianna, Morkell and Mareco; sisters, Cathy Rittenhouse of Forrest, IL. Nancy (George) Wallis of Boody, many cousins, nieces, nephews, family members and friends. Terry was preceded in death by his parents.

Services to celebrate Terry's life will be 1 PM Thursday, January 24, 2013 at Graceland/Fairlawn Funeral Home. Burial will be at Graceland Cemetery with Military Rites by the Macon County Honor Guard and conclude with the "Flight Home Ceremony." In lieu of flowers, please direct contributions to the Disabled Veterans of America.

The family of Terry L Woolums is being served by Graceland/ Fairlawn Funeral Home. Online condolences and memories may be shared with the family at www.gracelandfairlawn.com.

APPENDIX H

TRIBUTE TO PETER ZINK
WRITTEN BY MICHAEL DANKERT

Peter (Pete) Zink was one of our post-August 15 replacements. Pete was from Troy, New York. He had an eastern accent and, like all guys I've met from New York, liked to talk. I liked Pete immediately. He never went through that "FNG-Why Vietnam?" phase. Pete adjusted to Vietnam quickly. When the monsoons hit, while others stood around and grumbled Pete stuck an entrenching tool in the ground, centered his poncho over it, staked out the ends, crawled underneath and went to sleep. He did whatever he was asked to do. Pete said he had seen us receive commendations and decided that Sgt. Glyn and Sgt. Mike, as he called us, knew what they were doing, and he was going to follow along. He never complained. Once when we were on LZ 4-11 I felt bad because I had to assign him to a garbage detail. I checked on him later and Pete was all smiles. They let him drive a 3/4 ton truck to pick up the garbage, and he was ramrodding all over 4-11 picking up garbage and hauling it to the 4-11 dump. Another time I had to "tell" Pete and Manny Strauch to go to the 4-11 mess hall so that the Donut Dollies, who were visiting, had an audience of GIs to cheer up. Pete and Manny did their duty and learned how to fold paper to make paper whales.

My favorite memory of Pete is a time on 4-11. We were on the hill for Thanksgiving 1969. I wasn't feeling well enough to go the mess hall for Thanksgiving dinner so I stayed behind at the bunker. Pete brought me back a plate with turkey, potatoes, dressing and pie—the works. I ate while Pete opened a package he had gotten from home, from his family or his drinking buddy Tommy, I can't remember which. It's the only time I heard him complain. He started carrying on about a loaf of bread in the package. It was dried up and hard. He couldn't figure why someone sent him that. Why did they think he'd want a loaf of bread? And they should have known it wouldn't be any good by the time it got to him. Disgusted Pete took the box and put it in a trash barrel near our bunker. I finished my plate and went to throw it in the barrel and noticed something shiny. I pulled out the bread and found a bottle. Uncle Louie had carved out the bread so a small bottle of whiskey fit inside it. Apparently he thought the bread cushioned the bottle and keep it from breaking. I asked Pete if he was sure he didn't want the loaf of bread as I opened it and held up the bottle. He got a big smile on his face. Pete opened the bottle, and we raised a glass, actually canteen cups, and drank a toast.

The last time I saw Pete was in January 1970. He and Bill Davenport were wounded on January 14, the same date Gary Morris and Roger Kidwell were killed. Pete and Bill were medevacked to Chu Lai. I visited them in the hospital. An RPG had exploded near Pete. His face was a contorted mess. His face was bruised, swollen and cut. He could only see out of one eye. He drank using a straw through the corner of his mouth. He never complained or felt sorry for himself. He said not to worry about him; he was going home.

The last time I spoke to Pete was 1985. Terry Woolums had contacted us separately and told us about the Hill 4-11 reunion in St. Louis, Missouri. Pete called me. I recognized his voice immediately—that New York accent. He told me he had recovered from the wounds and had only a small scar on his face. We talked about what we had done after Vietnam. Pete was working in a small bar. Not a surprise, Pete was known to drink a few beers. He had gotten married and was divorced but still friendly with his ex. At one point in the conversation he said, "So are we going to do this thing?" meaning attend the 4-11 reunion. I said I will if you will. We agreed to meet in St. Louis. I went to the reunion but Pete never showed. Later I tried to call him without success. I never heard from him again.

A few years later I got a call and heard what I thought was a familiar voice. It was Ed Zink, Pete's brother. He had opened Pete's safe deposit box and found my name and phone number. Ed told me that Pete had died from cancer attributed to Agent Orange. As Pete was dying he asked his brother to contact me but Ed was unable to find my number. I missed the funeral but Ed gave me his address and I sent him money telling him to buy a round for the guys at the bar in memory of Pete.

GLOSSARY

Americal Division—This was unusual, as most U.S. divisions are known by a number. The Americal (23rd Infantry Division) was reactivated 25 September 1967 at Chu Lai in Vietnam from a combination of units already in Vietnam and newly arrived. The division was composed of the 11th, 196th, and 198th Light Infantry Brigades and divisional support units. Both the 11th and 198th brigades were newly formed units.[1]

AK-47—The Kalashnikov is an automatic or semiautomatic rifle that's gas operated and fed by a 30-round magazine of 7.62mm ammunition. Used by the North Vietnam Army soldiers and Viet Cong.[2]

AO—An Area of Operation is a geographical area, usually defined by boundaries such as mountains, rivers, and highways and assigned to a commander, by a higher commander, in which he has responsibility and the authority to conduct military operations.

APC—The Armored Personnel Carrier was the first modern "battle taxi"; developed to transport infantry forces on the mechanized battlefield. The main armament is a single .50 Cal heavy barrel machine gun, and the secondary armament is two M-60 machine guns. The vehicle is capable of "swimming" bodies of water.[3]

Bronze Star Medal with Valor—Is an individual military award of the United States Armed Forces. It may be awarded for acts of heroism, acts of merit, or meritorious service in a combat zone. The Bronze Star Medal is the fourth-highest individual military award and the ninth-highest by order of precedence in the US Military. When awarded for acts of heroism, the medal is awarded with the "V" device.[4]

C-130—The C-130 Hercules is a four-prop airplane that primarily performed the intra-theater part of the airlift mission. The aircraft can operate from rough, dirt strips and is the prime transport for troops and equipment into hostile areas. Basic and specialized versions perform a diversity of roles, including airlift support, gunship, aeromedical missions, and aerial spray missions, to name a few.[5]

C-4—Known as Composition, C-4 is a plastic explosive used by the military. Typically packaged in a one-and-a-quarter-pound block.

Chi-Com—A Chinese-Communist fragmentation hand grenade used by the VC and NVA.

Chinook—The CH-47 Chinook helicopter transports troops, artillery, supplies and equipment to the battlefield. Other applications include medical evacuation, aircraft recovery, parachute drop, search-and-rescue, disaster relief, firefighting, and heavy construction.[6]

Claymore Mine—Is a directional fragmentation mine, 8-1/2 inches long, 1-3/8 inches wide, 3-1/4 inches high, and weighs 3-1/2 pounds. The mine has 700 steel spheres (10.5 grains) and 1-1/2 pound layer of composition C-4 explosive and is initiated by an electric blasting cap. The M18 command-detonated mine may be used with obstacles or on the approaches, forward edges, flanks, and rear edges of protective minefields as close-in protection against a dismounted infantry attack.[7]

Cobra Attack Helicopter—The Cobra had two 7.62 multi-barrel mini-guns or two 40mm grenade launchers or one of each in the turret. When mixed, the mini-gun was on the right side.

Coke Girl—Vietnamese woman who sold Cokes and other products to GIs.

Command-detonated Bomb—Is an explosive device that the enemy placed, normally in a location that troops will move through. The device will have an electrical cord with a blasting cap attached to the explosive and a triggering device on the other end held by an enemy soldier. Once the trigger was pressed or clicked, the device would explode.

Concussion Grenade—Is designed to produce casualties during close combat while minimizing danger to friendly personnel. The grenade is also used for concussion effects in enclosed areas, for blasting, or for demolition tasks. The shock waves (over-pressure) produced by this grenade when used in enclosed areas are greater than those produced by the fragmentation grenade. It is, therefore, very effective against enemy soldiers in bunkers, buildings, and fortified areas.[8]

Dink—See Gook.

Dust-off—See UH-1 Huey Helicopter

FNG—Is a Fucking New Guy and a derogatory term used to identify the newest soldiers assigned to the platoon. The term was dropped for each soldier when they proved themselves or a newer soldier was assigned.

Frag—See Hand Grenade.

Free Fire Zone—Is a specifically designated area in which any weapons or weapon systems might fire without having to coordinate with the main headquarters. In general, free fire zone is an area where all friendly forces had been supposedly cleared, and any remaining people were hostile.[9]

FSB—The camps, called Fire Support Bases (FSB), provided a center of defense for the artillerymen and infantry troops operating in the area, protection for command and control personnel, a first-aid medical facility, and a relatively safe place for helicopters to land to resupply the FSB. Over time, the FSBs grew to become the central feature in many soldiers' lives. A FSB was built for one main purpose: to provide a base for field artillery to fire in support of infantry missions.[10]

Gook—A derogatory term for an NVA or Viet Cong soldier and used to reference civilians, too.

Grunt—A slang name for an infantry soldier.

Hand Grenade—Is a steel sphere designed to burst into many fragments when detonated. It produces casualties within an effective range of 49.5 feet (15 meters) by the high-velocity projection of fragments. The grenade body has 6.5 ounces of high explosive. Each grenade is fitted with a fuse that activates the explosive charge.[11]

Hedgerow—Shrubs and trees growing along and separating rice paddies or bordering a field.

Hooch—Is slang for a building with one to many rooms where soldiers lived. Referred to a Vietnamese home.

Humping—Term used to walk from one point to another while carrying all your equipment and weapon.

Jungle Rot—A sore or lesion developed when a soldier got a cut anywhere on the body, normally arms, feet, and legs from the elephant grass or thorns in the jungle growth. A fungus or bacterial infection develops.

KIA—Term for US service member Killed in Action.

Klick—A term used for a distance of one kilometer.

Leave—Was a one-time, seven-day leave, counted against your leave time, to a country outside of Vietnam. This allowed soldiers a second chance during a tour to get away and relax for a week. You normally flew standby when going on leave. Some destinations were Japan, Thailand, Philippines, Taiwan, Hawaii, and Australia.

Listening Post—A listening post (LP) is a position at night outside and forward of the platoon perimeter for early warning.

Logger—Is a temporary defensive perimeter set up by a unit, typically at night.

LZ—A landing zone is the location that the company or platoon assigned a mission that involves insertion by air assault. Also see FSB.

M-16 Rifle—Is a 5.56 millimeter caliber gas-operated, magazine-fed rifle for semi-automatic or automatic operation used by United States troops since the mid-1960s.[12]

M-60 Machine Gun—It fires the standard NATO 7.62 mm round and a general support crew-served weapon. It has a removable barrel that can be easily changed to prevent overheating. The weapon has an integral, folding bipod and can be mounted on a folding tripod.[13]

M-72 Light Anti-Tank Weapon (LAW)—Is a lightweight, self-contained, anti-armor weapon consisting of a rocket packed in a launcher. It is man-portable, may be fired from either shoulder, and is issued as a round of ammunition. It requires little from the user—only a visual inspection and operator maintenance. The launcher, which consists of two tubes, one inside the other, serves as a watertight packing container for the rocket and houses a percussion-type firing mechanism that activates the rocket.[14]

M-79 Grenade Launcher—Is a single-shot, break-open, shoulder-fired weapon. It is breech-loading and fires a 40mm grenade. It has an open, fixed front sight and an open, adjustable rear sight.[15]

MOS—The Army refers to specific jobs as Military Occupation Specialties. An example is an Infantryman job had an MOS of 11B.

MPC—Military Payment Certificates was the currency used by the US Military in Vietnam. US currency was not used or allowed in Vietnam. MPC was issued in the amounts of 5, 10, 25, and 50 cents, and 1, 5, 10, and 20 dollars. When going on R&R or leave, you would convert your MPC to dollars and, when returning, convert dollars back to MPC. When you returned to the States, MPC was converted to US dollars.

NVA—North Vietnam Army soldiers assigned to a specific unit.

Observation Post—An observation post (OP) is a position during daylight, outside and forward of the platoon perimeter for early warning.

Punji Stick (or Punji Stake)—Is a type of booby-trapped stake. It is a simple spike, made out of wood or bamboo, placed upright in the ground. Punji sticks are usually deployed in substantial numbers.

The stake itself will be sharpened and, in some cases, rubbed with toxic plants, frogs, or even feces, to cause infections in the wounded enemy.[16]

Purple Heart—Is awarded to members of the armed forces of the U.S. who are wounded by an instrument of war in the hands of the enemy and posthumously to the next of kin in the name of those who are killed in action or die of wounds received in action. It is specifically a combat decoration.[17]

R & R—Rest and Recuperation was a one-time, seven-day leave, not counted against your leave time, to a country outside of Vietnam. This allowed soldiers to get away and truly relax for a week. You had a reserved flight. Some destinations were Japan, Thailand, Philippines, Taiwan, Hawaii, and Australia.

Red Ball—Slang term for Highway 1 that ran north and south.

ROK—Republic of Korea Armed Forces soldiers assigned to a specific South Korean unit.

RTO—Radio Telephone Operator handles the maintenance and use of radio communication equipment. This equipment needs to always work in order for a platoon to communicate with other units. Typically an infantry soldier is assigned to the platoon leader and platoon sergeant for the RTO duties.

Satchel Charge—Is a demolition device, primarily intended for combat, whose primary components are a charge of dynamite or a more potent explosive such as C-4 plastic explosive, a carrying device functionally similar to a satchel or messenger bag, and a triggering mechanism; the term covers both improvised and formally designed devices.[18]

Shadow—See C-130.

Silver Star—Is the third-highest military combat decoration that can be awarded to a member of the United States Armed Forces. It is awarded for gallantry in action. Actions that merit the Silver Star must be of such a high degree that they are above those required for all other U.S. combat decorations but do not merit award of the

Medal of Honor or a Service Cross (Distinguished Service Cross, the Navy Cross, or the Air Force Cross).[19]

Spider Hole—Is military parlance for a camouflaged one-man foxhole, used for observation. A spider hole is typically a shoulder-deep, protective, round hole, often covered by a camouflaged lid, in which a soldier can stand and fire a weapon. A spider hole differs from a foxhole in that a foxhole is usually deeper and designed to emphasize cover rather than concealment.[20]

Spooky—An Air Force C-47 gunship armed with mini-guns; can drop flares.

Stand-down—This was the term used to indicate that a unit, normally company size, would leave the field and go to the Division firebase for three days. This allowed the soldiers to relax in a safe environment, shower, sleep on bunks, and eat real food.

Track—See APC.

Trip Flare—Provides early warning of infiltration of enemy troops or signaling.

UH-1 Huey Helicopter—Is the most used military helicopter. The Bell UH-1 series Iroquois, better known as the "Huey," arrived in Vietnam in 1963. Before the end of the conflict, more than 5,000 of these versatile aircraft were introduced into Southeast Asia. "Hueys" were used for Medevac, command and control, and air assault; to transport personnel and materiel; and as gunships.[21]

VC—Viet Cong are civilian sympathizers to the North Vietnam cause and fought for and alongside the NVA.

Ville—A term used for a Vietnamese village.

WIA—Term for US service member Wounded in Action.

NOTES

1. "23rd Infantry Division (United States)." Wikipedia. Wikimedia Foundation, n.d. Web. 09 Apr. 2016. <https://en.wikipedia.org/wiki/23rd_Infantry_Division_(United_States)>.

2. "AK-47." Wikipedia. Wikimedia Foundation, n.d. Web. 09 Apr. 2016. <https://en.wikipedia.org/wiki/AK-47>.

3. "M113A1 Armored Personnel Carrier." M113A1 Armored Personnel Carrier. N.p., n.d. Web. 09 Apr. 2016. <http://fas.org/man/dod-101/sys/land/m113.htm>.

4. "Bronze Star Medal –." Army Live. N.p., n.d. Web. 18 Aug. 2016. <http://armylive.dodlive.mil/index.php/2014/02/bronze-star-medal-heroic-or-meritorious-achievement-or-service/>.

5. "C-130 Hercules."—Military Aircraft. N.p., n.d. Web. 09 Apr. 2016. <http://fas.org/man/dod-101/sys/ac/c-130.htm>.

6. "CH-47D/F/MH-47E Chinook Helicopter." Army Technology. N.p., n.d. Web. 09 July 2016. <http://www.army-technology.com/projects/chinook/>."

7. M18 Claymore." M18 Claymore. N.p., n.d. Web. 09 Apr. 2016. <http://fas.org/man/dod-101/sys/land/m18-claymore.htm>.

8. "MK3A2 Concussion Offensive Hand Grenade." MK3A2 Concussion Offensive Hand Grenade. N.p., n.d. Web. 09 Apr. 2016. <http://fas.org/man/dod-101/sys/land/mk3a2.htm>.

9. N.p., n.d. Web. <http://thevietnamwar.info/free-fire-zone/>.

10. "Fire Support Base." Wikipedia. Wikimedia Foundation, n.d. Web. 09 Apr. 2016. <https://en.wikipedia.org/wiki/Fire_support_base>.

11. "M61 Fragmentation Hand Grenade." M61 Fragmentation Hand Grenade. N.p., n.d. Web. 09 Apr. 2016. <http://fas.org/man/dod-101/sys/land/m61.htm>.

12. "M16A2 5.56mm Semiautomatic Rifle." M16A2 5.56mm Semiautomatic Rifle. N.p., n.d. Web. 07 Apr. 2016. <http://fas.org/man/dod-101/sys/land/m16.htm>.

13. "M60E3 7.62mm Machine Gun." M60E3 7.62mm Machine Gun. N.p., n.d. Web. 09 Apr. 2016. <http://fas.org/man/dod-101/sys/land/m60e3.htm>.

14. "M-72 Light Anti-tank Weapon (LAW)." M-72 Light Anti-tank Weapon (LAW). N.p., n.d. Web. 09 Apr. 2016. <http://fas.org/man/dod-101/sys/land/m72.htm>.

15. "M79 Grenade Launcher." Wikipedia. Wikimedia Foundation, n.d. Web. 09 Apr. 2016. <https://en.wikipedia.org/wiki/M79_grenade_launcher>.

16. "Punji Stick." Wikipedia. Wikimedia Foundation, n.d. Web. 09 Apr. 2016. <https://en.wikipedia.org/wiki/Punji_stick>.

17. "History of the Order." Military Order of the Purple Heart. N.p., n.d. Web. 18 Aug. 2016. <http://www.purpleheart.org/HistoryOrder.aspx>.

18. "Satchel Charge." Wikipedia. Wikimedia Foundation, n.d. Web. 09 Apr. 2016. <https://en.wikipedia.org/wiki/Satchel_charge>.

19. "Military Awards for Valor—Top 3." Description of Awards. N.p., n.d. Web. 18 Aug. 2016. <http://valor.defense.gov/Description-of-Awards/>.

20. "Spider Hole." Wikipedia. Wikimedia Foundation, n.d. Web. 18 Aug. 2016. <https://en.wikipedia.org/wiki/Spider_hole>.

21. "UH-1 Huey Helicopter."—Military Aircraft. N.p., n.d. Web. 09 Apr. 2016. <http://fas.org/man/dod-101/sys/ac/uh-1.htm>.

ABOUT THE AUTHOR

Glyn Haynie has been married to his patient wife Sherrie for 29 years and has five children, 13 grandchildren, and two great-grandchildren. He served 20 years in the Army, retiring March 1, 1989. After retirement, he completed his BS degree in Computer Information Systems and an MA in Computer Resources and Information Systems. He worked as a software engineer/project manager for eight years and then taught for Park University as a full-time instructor and as an adjunct instructor for 13 years. He is currently retired.

Figure 61 Glyn Haynie. Photograph by Shannon Prothro Photography.

Author's Website http://www.glynhaynie.net

I hope you enjoyed this book. Would you do me a favor?

Like all authors, I rely on online reviews, and your opinion is invaluable. Would you take a few moments now to share your assessment of my book on Amazon or any other book review website you prefer? Your opinion will help the book marketplace become more transparent and useful to all.

Thank you very much!

CPSIA information can be obtained
at www.ICGtesting.com
Printed in the USA
LVHW081356101220
673836LV00042B/790